IVAN MOSCOVICH

Fiendishly Frustrating
Brain-Twisting Puzzles

Sterling Publishing Co., Inc.
New York

Fiendishly Frustrating Brain-Twisting Puzzles
Was commissioned, edited,
designed, and produced by
Imagine Puzzles Ltd.,
20 Lochaline Street
London W6 9SH
United Kingdom

Managing director: **Hal Robinson**
Editor: **Alison Moore**
Project manager: **Tamiko Rex**
Art editor: **Beatriz Waller**
Copy editor: **Ruth Binney**
Illustrations: **Beatriz Waller**

Library of Congress Cataloging-in-Publication Data Available

10 9 8 7 6 5 4 3 2 1

Published by Sterling Publishing Co., Inc.
387 Park Avenue South, New York, NY 10016
by arrangement with Imagine Puzzles Ltd, London
All puzzles © Ivan Moscovich
Artwork and text © 2004 by Imagine Puzzles Ltd.
Material in this volume previously appeared in *Fiendishly Difficult
Math Puzzles* and *Fiendishly Difficult Visual Perception Puzzles*
Distributed in Canada by Sterling Publishing
C/o Canadian Manda Group, 165 Dufferin Street
Toronto, Ontario, Canada M6K 3H6
Distributed in Great Britain by Chrysalis Books Group PLC
The Chrysalis Building, Bramley Road, London W10 6SP, England
Distributed in Australia by Capricorn Link (Australia) Pty. Ltd.
P.O. Box 704, Windsor, NSW 2756, Australia

Printed in China
All rights reserved

Sterling ISBN 1-4027-1809-8

Contents

Introduction 4

How to solve problems 5

Sample games 6

Match blocks 8

Finding the key 10

Continuous paths 12

Sliding coins 14

Magic numbers 1 16

Magic numbers 2 18

Combi-cards 20

Money problems 22

The 18-point problem 24

Jumping coins 26

Life or death 28

From pillar to post 30

Gridlock 32

Crossroads 33

Separate and connect 34

The Tower of Brahma 36

Interplanetary courier 38

Husbands and wives 40

The octopus handshake 42

Calculating the odds 44

Up in the air 46

Lucky spinner, lucky dice 48

Hidden shapes 50

Match the lines 52

Square the match 53

Tracks and traces 54

Count the cubes 56

Dividing the square 58

Cube problems 60

Pegboards 61

Inside-outside 62

Repli-tiles 1 64

Repli-tiles 2 66

On the rebound 68

A piece of cake 70

The hollow cube 72

How many? 74

Cubes and routes 76

Find the polygons 78

Multi-views 80

Distortrix 1 82

Distortrix 2 84

Space filler 86

Subways 88

Computer patterns 90

Answers 93

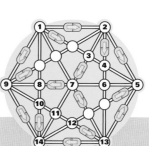

Introduction

I have always been fascinated by puzzles and games for the mind. I enjoy brain games of all types— particularly those with some special aspect or feature. The ones I like most are not always the hardest: Sometimes a puzzle that is quite easy to solve has an elegance or a "meaning" behind it that makes it especially satisfying. I have tried to provide a good selection in this book: Some are easy and some are fiendishly difficult, but they are all tremendous fun! Above all, I have tried to provide something for everyone, in order to share my delight in such puzzles and games as widely as possible.

Solving puzzles has as much to do with the way you approach them as with natural ability or any impersonal measure of intelligence. Most people should be able to solve nearly all the puzzles in this book, although of course some will seem easier than others. All it takes are common sense, a practical approach, a bit of logic, and— occasionally—a little persistence or a flash of insight.

Thinking is what it's all about: Comprehension is at least as important as visual perception or mathematical knowledge. After all, it is our different *ways* of thinking that set us apart as individuals and make each of us unique.

Although some of us feel we are better at solving problems mathematically, and others prefer to tackle problems involving similarities and dissimilarities, and yet others simply proceed by trial-and-error persistence, we all have a very good chance of solving a broad selection of puzzles, as I'm sure you will find as you tackle those in this book.

From long and happy experience, however, I can tell you one secret, one golden rule: When you look at a puzzle, no matter how puzzling it seems, simply believe you can solve it, and sure enough, you will!

IVAN MOSCOVICH

How to solve problems

To get things going, let's look at the different approaches that can be useful in solving puzzles.

First, the logical approach. Logic is always valuable, as it helps you work things out sequentially, using information received to progress step by step to the answer. This is especially true in games of *chance*, which tend to be oriented toward mathematics and concentrate on using numbers for simple calculations, or on ordering arrangements of objects or figures. Examples of this can be found in the *magic numbers* puzzles on pages 16–19.

In problem-solving, there may also be a need for an indirect approach, whereby you arrive at an answer by perceiving and thinking about a subject in a way you have never done before. This depends on how you think normally, of course, but such lateral thinking will prove a valuable tool for many of the *chance* and *shape* puzzles in this book. The first part of *Match blocks* on pages 8–9, for example, is solved most simply, quickly, easily, and elegantly using an indirect approach of this kind.

The visual approach is also important, especially in the *shape* puzzles, because every puzzle is presented in visual terms and requires initial visual comprehension (or conceptualization) combined with a clear understanding of the challenge being set.

This is particularly the case with *count the cubes* on pages 56–57.

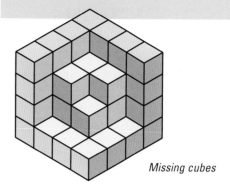
Missing cubes

In general, the puzzles in this book are concerned with different skills and approaches to puzzle-solving, including:

1 simple calculation using patterns, objects, or symbols;

2 spotting serial links and connections;

3 using the laws of chance and probability—particularly in assessing the odds for or against specific events or results occurring;

4 ordering, combining, or grouping objects or figures, following a defined rule, to achieve a stated target;

5 applying logic to problems that may at first seem to defy a logical approach;

6 awareness of spatial relationships, using a combination of observation and imagination to identify key components.

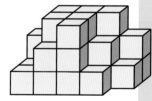
Count the cubes

See if you can solve the sample games on pages 6–7 first without looking at the answers—then go on to enjoy the rest of the book! If you have any queries about any of the puzzles, or you would just like to get in touch, please write to me care of the publishers. I shall be pleased to hear from you.

Magic wheel

Seven-pointed star

Sample games

It's time to prepare your mind for the games that follow. To start you off, you'll find a selection of sample puzzles below, some of which may be familiar. I don't want you to burn out too quickly, so I've given you the answers too. But I haven't been so kind elsewhere in the book . . .

Game 1

Here is a mental jigsaw puzzle. Nine of the 12 numbered squares below make up the larger square. Which squares fit where, and which three are redundant? The squares are not necessarily the right way up.

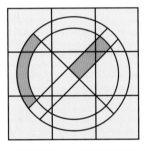

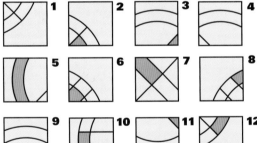

Game 2

Two coins lie side by side. If the coin on the left is rolled around the coin on the right, in which direction will the head be facing when it reaches the other side? (This requires either a vivid imagination or a little mathematical knowledge.)

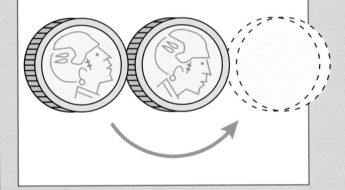

ANSWER 2

Although many people believe the coin would then be upside down, in fact it is right side up: The coin has traveled halfway round the other—but has turned a full circle.

ANSWER 1

12	3	6		2
5	7	11		4
8	9	1		10

Game 3

The magic square is possibly the oldest mathematical puzzle in existence. Examples have been found dating back to before 2000 B.C. By 900 A.D. one Arab treatise was even recommending that pregnant women should wear a charm marked with a magic square for a favorable birth.

Can you distribute the numbers 1 through 16 in this 4 x 4 square so that lines across, lines down, and major diagonals all add up to the same total?

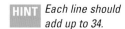 **HINT** *Each line should add up to 34.*

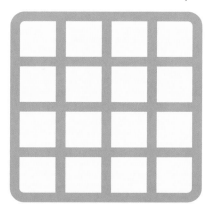

Game 4

In a darkened room there is a box of mixed gloves: 5 blue pairs, 4 red pairs, and 2 white pairs. You find the box by feeling for it. How many gloves must you take out—without being able to see them—to make sure you have two of the same color?

And how many must you take out to make sure you have both the left and right hand of the same color?

ANSWER 3

There are quite a few possible arrangements for these numbers: For example, if you reverse the rows horizontally or vertically the answer is the same. This solution, therefore, is just one of many.

16	3	2	13
5	10	11	8
9	6	7	12
4	15	14	1

ANSWER 4

To be certain you have two gloves of the same color you must take out four gloves—one more than the number of different colors.

To be certain you have a matched pair—both left and right hand of the same color—you must take out 12 gloves: one more than the total number of gloves for one or other hand.

Match blocks

The blocks in columns on these two pages can be arranged in a 7 x 7 square formation so that the horizontal rows are numbered in some order from 1 through 7, as shown in its simplest form in the diagram on the right.

ANSWERS PAGE 94

HINT *You can make your own set of blocks if you like, but a pencil, some thought, and the grid below should suffice.*

Game 1

The aim here is very simple. Rearrange the columns so that no number appears more than once in any horizontal row or vertical column. (This should not take long.)

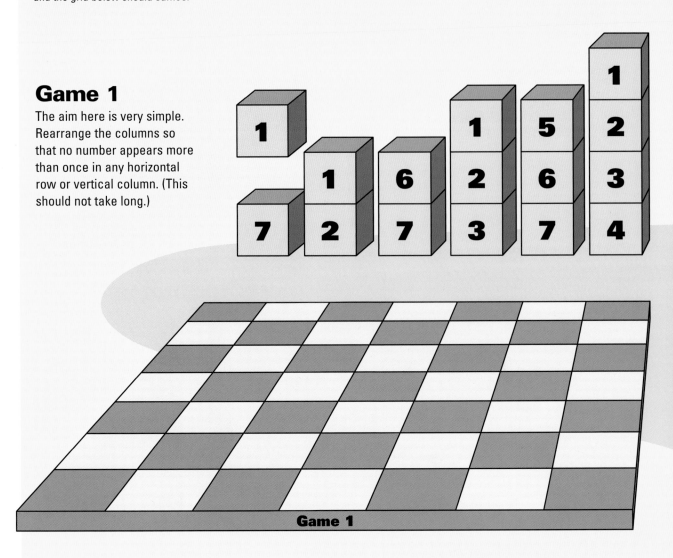

Game 1

8

Game 2

Arrange the columns again so that no number appears more than once, neither in a horizontal or vertical row nor in a large or small diagonal.

Game 2

Finding the key

Most of us carry a few keys around with us; some, like me, carry vast collections weighing down their pockets. It's not surprising, really, in view of the number of different things we now need to keep locked: automobiles, suitcases and briefcases, office doors and safes, even desks and bureaus at home...So here are a couple of puzzles on the subject— I hope you'll find the key to solving them.

ANSWERS PAGE 94

Keys to the keys

On a circular keyring there are ten keys, all with round handles, in a specific order that you have memorized. Each fits one of ten different locks. The trouble is, it's pitch dark: You can't see the keyring, you can only feel the keys with your fingers.

If you had some way of telling in the dark which key was which, it wouldn't take you long to find any particular one you wanted. So you decide to give some keys different-shaped tops—but do you need ten different tops?

What is the fewest different key tops you'll need to be sure, once you've felt them, that you've identified where you are on the ring? And would you put all the new keys together or give them some sort of arrangement?

HINT *Any symmetrical number or arrangement of keys will not help: You will still not know which way round you are holding the keyring. Use a pencil to mark the different shapes of key top to work out the solution. We've suggested some examples on the right.*

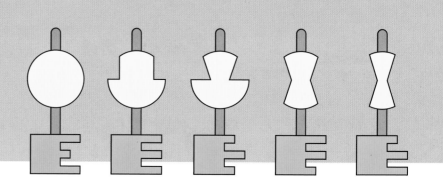

Combination lock

A safe has ten locks in combination, requiring ten keys, each of which bears a letter inscribed on its handle. But to confuse thieves some of the letters are the same.

The safe opens only when all the keys have been inserted in the locks, the handles then spelling out a secret code word.

Fortunately, you have a diagram of the interior of the locks, showing the shapes of the appropriate keys. Otherwise you might have to spend a lot of time trying out all the 3.6 million possible combinations of ten locks. And of course you also know the secret code word...

What is the secret code word?

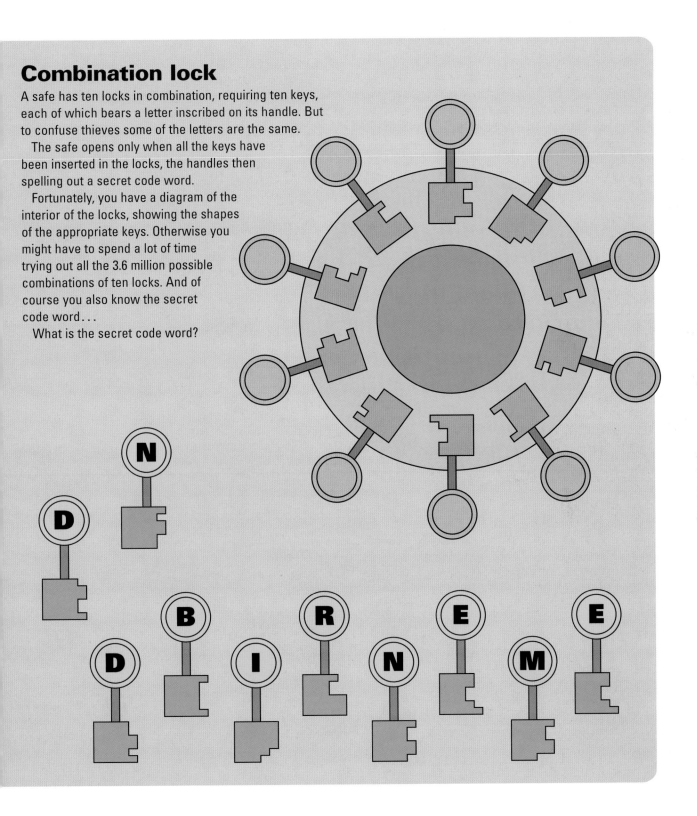

Continuous paths

Fifteen lines join the six points, or nodes, of a regular hexagon. Where each line crosses another there is a further node, giving a total of 19 nodes in all. Every line also carries an arrow: No matter where the arrow is located on this line, it makes the *whole* line directional.

ANSWERS PAGE 95

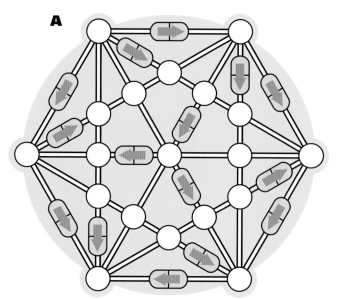

A

Sample game

The sample game shown below proves that it is not so easy: An unlucky or unskilful player may reach a node from which he or she is then unable to move farther because the arrows are contrary. Yet it may be that only a single move—but a wrong one—has foxed the player. In this case the player is unable to move beyond node 14, so five nodes remain blank.

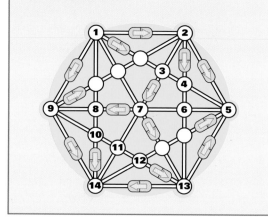

The object is to find a continuous path connecting all 19 nodes, starting anywhere (the start becomes node number 1, and the next is number 2, etc.). You must always travel down lines—or parts of lines—in the direction of the arrow, and you may visit each node only once. A (above) has arrows that point the same way as on the sample game. Can you complete it? Is there more than one node from which you can start? B, C, and D have arrows pointing in different directions. Can you find your way around all 19 nodes in each? Game B can end at only one node: Which one, and why?

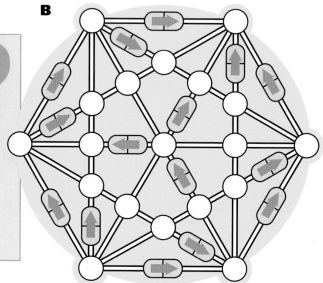

B

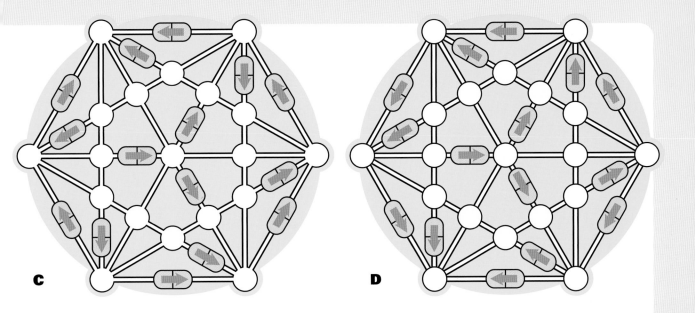

C   D

Devise your own

Arrows should point in one direction only. In the hexagons below (E and F), however, all the arrows are two-headed, because I am giving you a chance—*before* you start playing—to make up your own mind which direction you want the arrows to point. Shade off lightly in pencil the unwanted end of each arrow. Then play the game as usual.

This version of the game can also be played by two people, each taking turns to shade an arrow (until there are no more arrows) and make a move; the last to move is the winner. The decision about which way each arrow points can also be determined by chance: Toss a coin for each arrow—heads points left, tails points right.

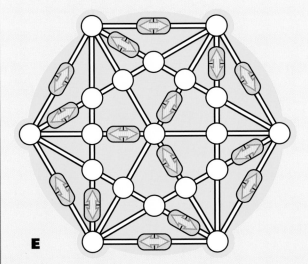

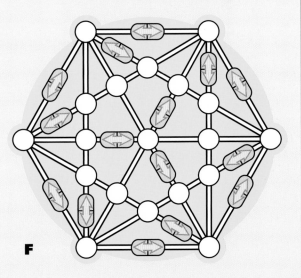

E   F

Sliding coins

In these games, I challenge you to reverse the positions of sets of coins within a confined space. Cash-flow problems, you might say! If you can't find coins of the right size, counters will do. Small circles in the game bases show the centers of the possible positions of coins or counters; the miniature diagrams indicate the starting positions for the games. One move involves moving a piece from its position to a free space; this need not be an adjacent space, but it must be reached without any other piece being disturbed. Jumping over other coins is not allowed.

ANSWERS PAGE 96

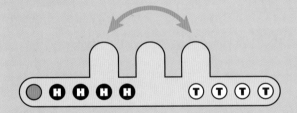

Game 1

Start with nine coins: four one way up (heads; black), four the other (tails; white), and one coin altogether different (red). If you use counters, choose different colors. By moving pieces one at a time into available free spaces, can you rearrange all the pieces to reverse the starting pattern?

What is the fewest number of moves required to complete the reversal? Can you do better than 36?

HINT *All three games can be played more easily if you construct (out of card, perhaps) bases of the shapes shown, in and on which coins can slide. Solving the problems mentally is a more interesting challenge, however.*

14

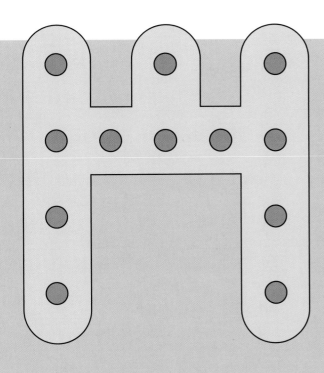

Game 2

This game requires only eight coins: four one way up (white) and four the other (black). But it is not necessarily easier—fewer coins are compensated for by less space in which to move.

What is the fewest number of moves in which you can reverse the positions of the two sets of four coins? Can you do better than 30?

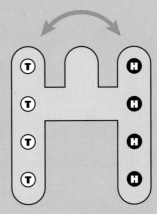

Game 3

In this game it is the starting and ending *space* that is the linear element, and it is all too easy to block everything with coins all trying to get past each other.

What is the fewest number of moves in which you can reverse the positions of the two sets of three coins successfully? Can you beat 15?

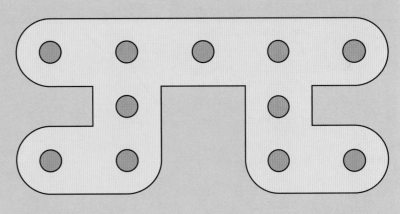

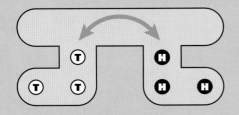

Magic numbers 1

Magic squares—in which lines of numbers add up to the same total whether read horizontally or vertically, or sometimes even diagonally—have been the delight of magicians (and mathematicians) throughout history. Yet many other shapes can be used equally well, if not better. Some are actually simpler—like the magic cross below. In most puzzles on these two pages, I have given you the total to which all the lines should add up—the "magic number." With or without the magic number, can you fill in the required spaces in each line?

ANSWERS PAGE 97

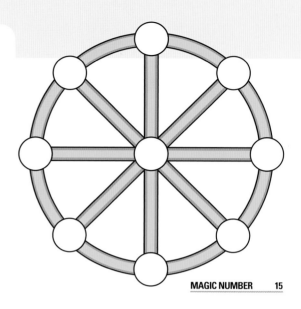

MAGIC NUMBER   15

Magic cross

The magic cross below is only part of a magic square. Can you insert the numbers 1 through 12 in the squares so that the four lines of four squares across and down all total the magic number?

MAGIC NUMBER   26

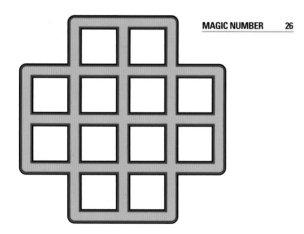

Magic wheel

In the magic wheel above, can you distribute the numbers 1 through 9 around the nodes so that lines across the wheel—from outer node to the center node and on to the opposite outer node— all add to the magic number?

Magic hexagon

In the magic hexagon, can you distribute the numbers 1 through 13 around the nodes so that lines—from the outer node to the center node and on to the opposite outer node, and also along each side—reach the magic total?

 **HINT** *Look for the key center number.*

MAGIC NUMBER   21

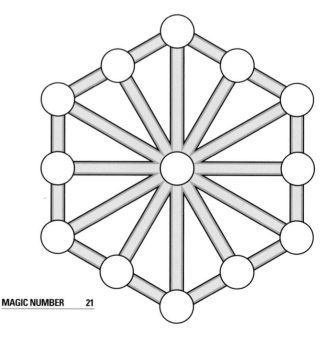

16

Six-point star

Magic stars are based upon hexagons, heptagons, and octagons. In the six-point star, can you distribute the numbers 1 through 12 around the nodes so that each of the six lines adds up to the magic number in the middle?

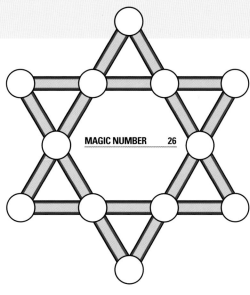

MAGIC NUMBER   26

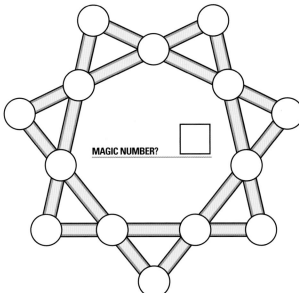

MAGIC NUMBER?

Seven-point star

In the seven-point star, can you distribute the numbers 1 through 14 around the nodes so that each of the seven lines adds up to the same total? No magic number is given.

HINT *Find a relationship between the highest number inserted in the six-point star and its magic number, and you may be able to calculate the magic number for the seven-point star.*

Eight-point star

In the eight-point star, can you distribute the numbers 1 through 16 around the nodes so that each of the eight lines adds up to the same total? Again, no magic number is given (but see the hint above).

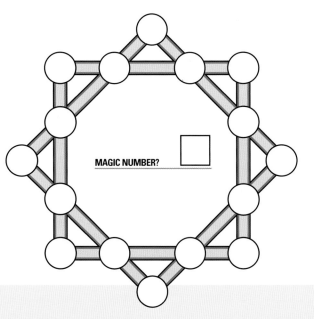

MAGIC NUMBER?

Magic numbers 2

These magic squares are all slightly more complex than the other magic shapes in the book, even though they are merely squares. That is because some entail more than just addition, or I have put in some other restriction or condition affecting your choice to perplex you.

ANSWERS PAGE 98

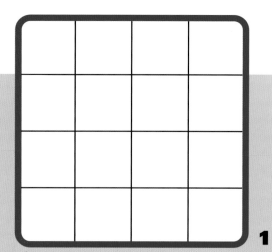

1 In this 4 x 4 magic square, can you distribute the numbers

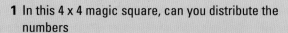

8 7 6 5 4 3 2 1

-1 -2 -3 -4 -5 -6 -7 -8

so that the lines across, lines down, and the two main diagonals all total zero?

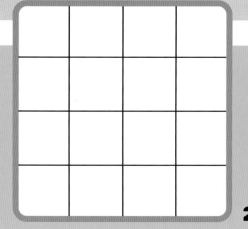

2 Now let's add a zero to the numbers to be distributed:

8 7 6 5 4 3 2 1

0 -1 -2 -3 -4 -5 -6 -7

This time all the lines actually add up to a positive number. Which number?

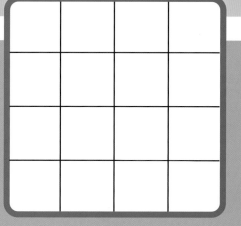

3 Continuing this theme, can you distribute the numbers:

12 11 10 9 8 7 6 5

4 3 2 1 0 -1 -2 -3

so that the lines across, lines down, and the two main diagonals all total the same number? What is the total?

4

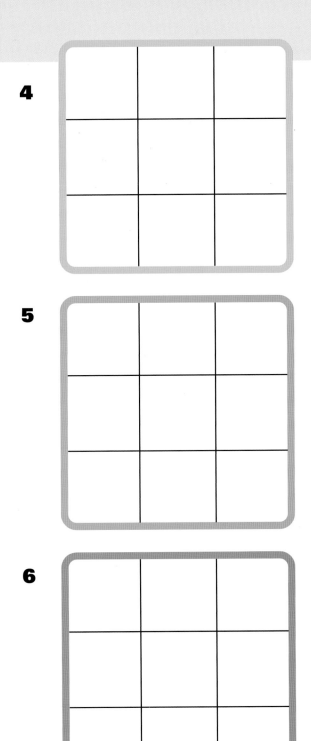

5

6

4 Let's turn now to a 3 x 3 magic square. First, can you distribute the numbers 1 through 9 in such a way that by subtracting the central number in any line of three from the sum of the outer two, all total the same, whether horizontally, vertically, or diagonally?

5 Next, can you distribute the numbers

1 2 3 4 6 9 12 18 36

in such a way that all the lines across, lines down, and diagonals, when multiplied internally, total the same number?

6 Now, can you distribute those identical numbers

1 2 3 4 6 9 12 18 36

in such a way that, by dividing the central number in any line of three into the product (after multiplication) of the outer two, the lines all total the same horizontally, vertically, and diagonally?

7 Finally, here's a 5 x 5 magic square with some internal squares shaded. Can you distribute the numbers 1 through 25 in such a way that the lines across, lines down, and the two main diagonals all add to the same total—and only odd numbers appear in the shaded squares?

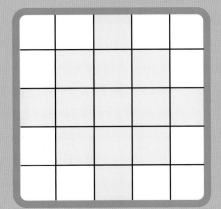

7

Combi-cards

Combi-cards are a bit like families: Every member is quite individual, yet each one has some feature that is strongly reminiscent of another—so that in each, some of the others are combined.

ANSWERS PAGE 99

Four cards

Sample game

1 2 | 1 3 | 2 3

In these three combi-cards, each card has two numbers, one of which appears on one of the other cards, and the other on the other. (The set thus has a total of three numbers, each featured twice.)

Five cards

Six cards

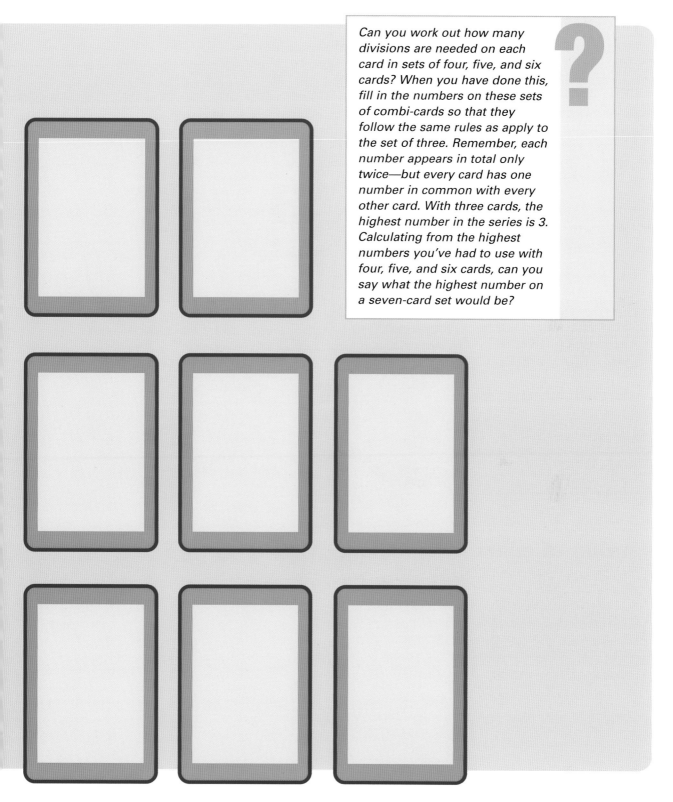

Can you work out how many divisions are needed on each card in sets of four, five, and six cards? When you have done this, fill in the numbers on these sets of combi-cards so that they follow the same rules as apply to the set of three. Remember, each number appears in total only twice—but every card has one number in common with every other card. With three cards, the highest number in the series is 3. Calculating from the highest numbers you've had to use with four, five, and six cards, can you say what the highest number on a seven-card set would be?

Money problems

I find playing with money is always a chancy thing, even if you are only using coins as counters, as in the puzzles on these two pages. The first game involves rearrangement. The second and third are like board games, with a difference...

ANSWERS PAGE 100

A ring of coins

Arrange six coins as shown: One is trapped in the middle of a nearly complete ring of coins. How can you slide the coins, one at a time, so as to get the trapped one out to the edge, and so complete the ring? Here's the catch: Each coin moved must end up touching two others, and no other coins may be disturbed. But you can take as many moves to do this as you like!

 Coins not being moved may be left touching only one other coin.

Solitaire 1

Place nine coins on the board opposite, leaving any one space free. Coins are removed by being jumped by another coin—every time one coin jumps its neighbor to land in an empty space, the jumped coin is removed; if the jumping coin can then jump a second or even a third coin, this is still part of the same move.

How many moves must you make to leave only one coin? Can you do it in fewer than six moves?

Solitaire 2

Now try the game with 14 coins on the board to the right: Leave space 4 free. In my best sequence I cleared the board of all but my jumping coin in nine moves—how about you? Why is it a good idea to start from space 4? Can you start from any other space and still clear the board successfully?

There are in fact only two other spaces to start from and succeed ... which ones?

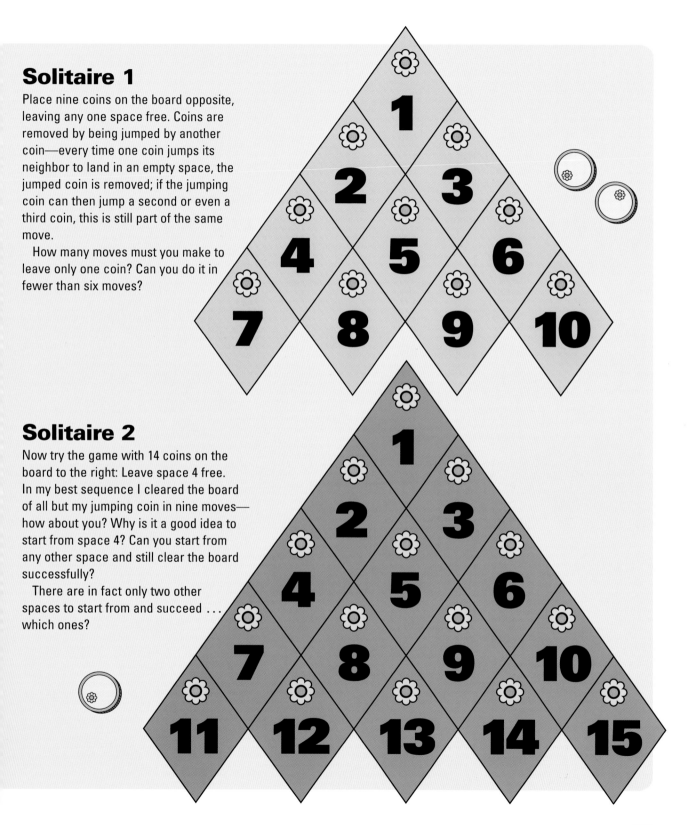

23

The 18-point problem

This problem is all about locating fixed points in spaces that change dimension. Imagine you have a long strip of land in which there is a tree. Dividing the land into halves, you plant another tree in the second half. Then you decide to divide your land again, and plant another tree. And again. And again. Each time, the trees already planted turn out, luckily, to be in their own separate plots.

Can you be foresighted—and farsighted—enough to plant your trees where they will be by themselves no matter how often you divide your land into equal parts?

The strip of land is represented here by a line, and the trees as dots or points.

ANSWERS PAGE 101

Think ahead

To give you some ideas about the methods—and the traps—in doing the puzzle, here we show an attempt that ended in failure at the fifth level: Points 2 and 4 are in the same new area. Can you complete the 11-line grid below, following the principles outlined, so that on the 11th level all 11 points (or trees) added serially are in their own plots?

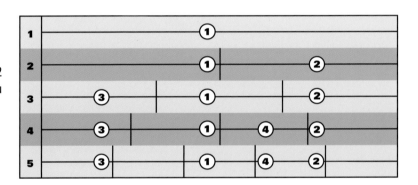

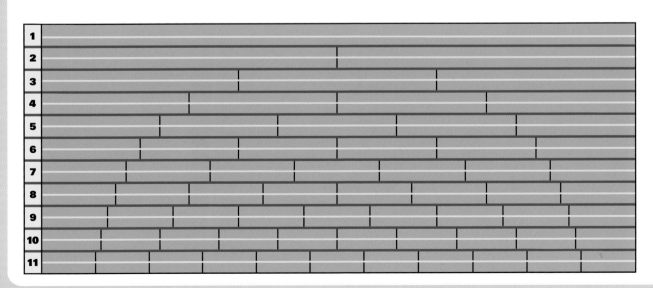

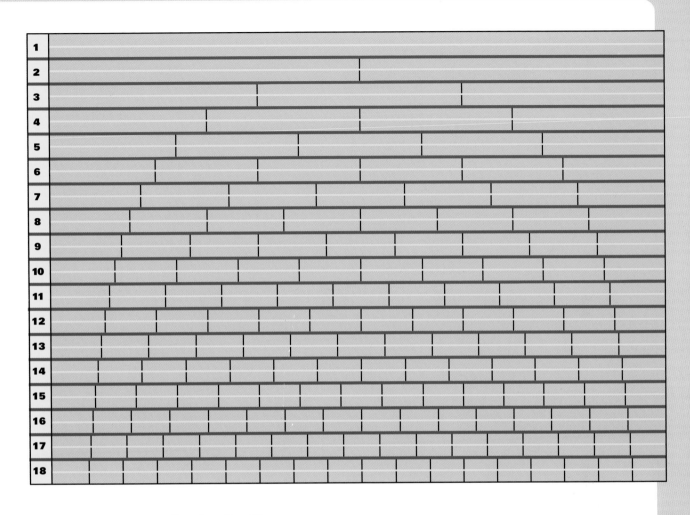

The open-ended challenge

You might imagine that, with sufficient foresight, the number of possible plots and trees within them (following the principles outlined) ought to approach the infinite. That is actually not the case: The limiting factors are the serial nature of the way points are added, and the permanence of the points once sited. But it is quite possible to break the 11th-division barrier—although, once more to emphasize foresight, the strategy to achieve 11 divisions may be totally different from one to make (say) 17.

How far can you get?

Jumping coins

For this game you need two sets of small coins, or counters, in contrasting colors. With coins, use one set showing heads, the other showing tails. The object of the puzzle is to reverse the pattern by exchanging the positions of the two sets of coins or counters within the coin "holders" shown. There are four rules you have to observe:

• Only one coin may be moved at a time.
• A coin may move into an adjacent empty space.
• A coin may jump over one of the *opposite type* into a space immediately beyond it.
• A coin may *not* jump over another of its own type.

ANSWERS PAGES 101–102

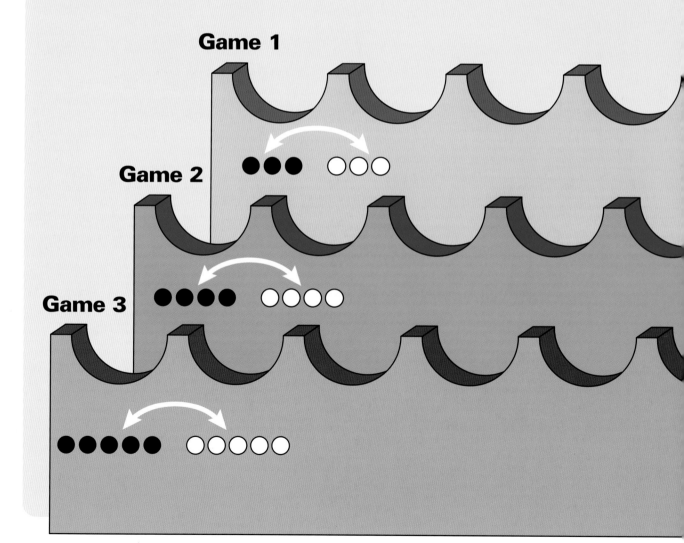

What is the minimum number of moves required to reverse the pattern with:

A Four coins, two of each type? This game is shown (Sample game, right). Answer: eight moves.

B Six coins, three of each type? (See the board plan, Game 1.)

C Eight coins, four of each type (Game 2)?

D Ten coins, five of each type (Game 3)?

Sample game

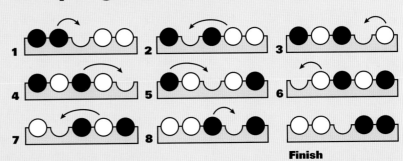

Can you spot a mathematical link between the first three solutions (to Sample, Game 1, and Game 2) that will give you the fourth solution (to Game 3) without your having to go through all the moves?

Life or death

Have you ever been in a situation where you have had to appear impartial when making a choice among a number of people? I have, and I know that, human nature being what it is, it's sometimes very difficult to suppress the urge to fix the odds for or against specific choices.

Elimination games depend on an apparently regular, and therefore impartial, selection that nevertheless realizes the desired (and distinctly partial) result. The games shown here are examples.

ANSWERS PAGE 103

Outer ring

Would you like to be emperor of Ancient Rome? I'm sure you would. The only problem is that 39 of your friends and acquaintances would like to be emperor too. Can you think of a fair and democratic way to eliminate all the competition so that only you and one other candidate (an obvious no-hoper) are left—at which time you can ensure all those eliminated vote for you?

Arrange everyone as in the large outer ring on these two pages, and employ the "old Roman custom" (which you've just invented) of selection by removing every third candidate (so number three is the first to go) and continuing as many times around the circle as necessary. At which numbers in the circle should you and your chosen co-finalist stand to be sure that you both remain when everyone else has been eliminated?

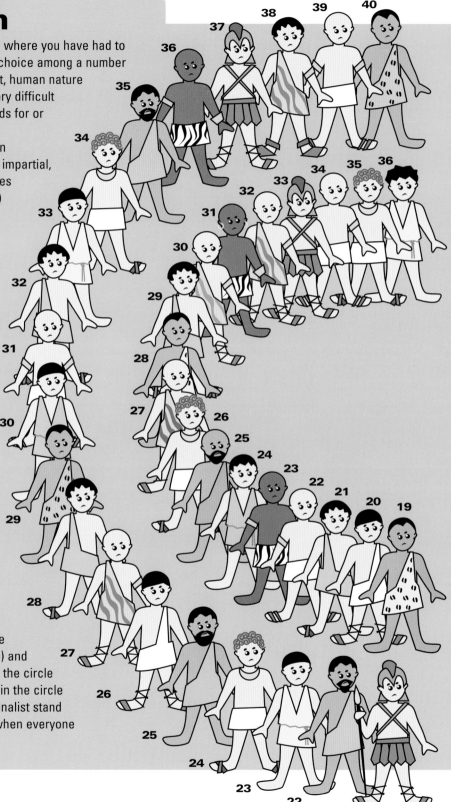

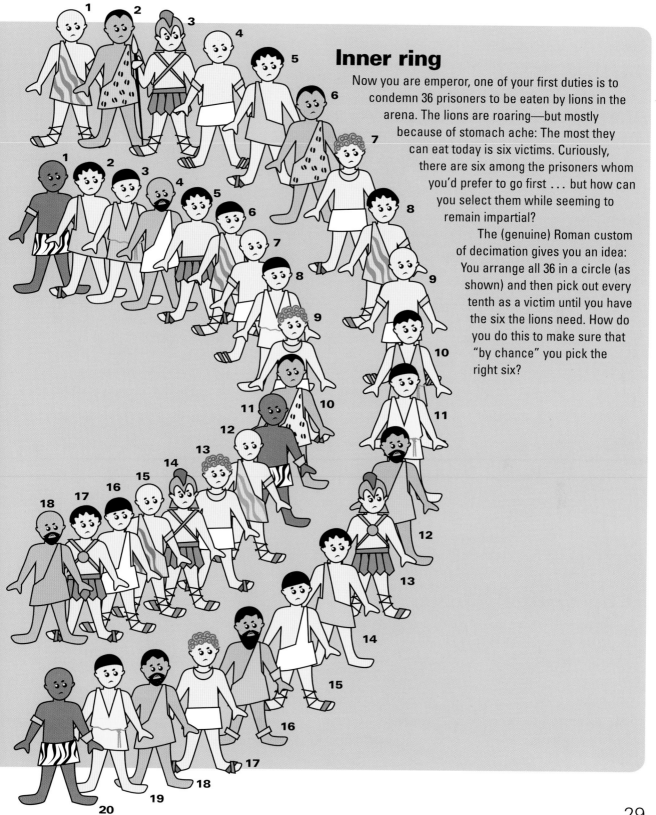

Inner ring

Now you are emperor, one of your first duties is to condemn 36 prisoners to be eaten by lions in the arena. The lions are roaring—but mostly because of stomach ache: The most they can eat today is six victims. Curiously, there are six among the prisoners whom you'd prefer to go first ... but how can you select them while seeming to remain impartial?

The (genuine) Roman custom of decimation gives you an idea: You arrange all 36 in a circle (as shown) and then pick out every tenth as a victim until you have the six the lions need. How do you do this to make sure that "by chance" you pick the right six?

From pillar to post

When I was young I used to play in a small, enclosed courtyard that had eight pillars around the outside. In the middle was an octagonal flowerbed with a low surrounding fence. I played a game in which I tried to run from pillar to pillar for as long as possible without repeating my track. I could cross my previous tracks and even hop over the fence and run across the flowerbed if necessary (if my father wasn't looking). But there was one rule: If the only track left from one pillar to any other led down one side of the octagonal fence, the game ended.

ANSWERS PAGE **103**

Sample game

This is an example of one attempt. I could travel to a pillar any number of times as long as each time it was from another direction and as long as I left again in a new direction. In this try, though, after my 13th move the only track left was down the side of the fence, and so I lost.

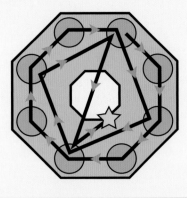

Courtyard challenge

How many moves can you make before you too are blocked? There are four outlines for you to play on.

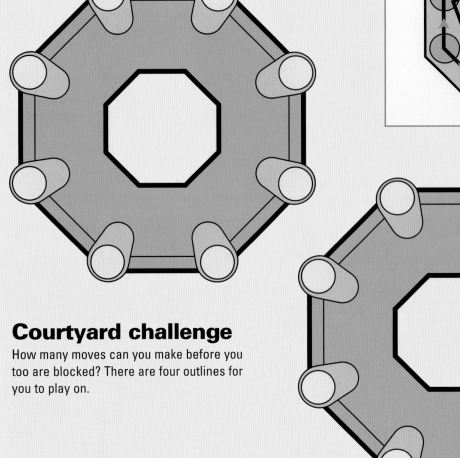

Posting the mail

At the center of a circular housing complex near where I live stands the communal mailbox—13 boxes on a central pillar. A pair of twins, known locally as Left and Right, deliver newspapers in the area, and they habitually play a game with the mailboxes. Each in turn slots a newspaper either into one mailbox only or into two adjacent mailboxes: The winner is the one who slots a newspaper into the last available box or boxes.

Using your left and right hands (and a pencil if you need to) and starting with your left, can you devise a strategy by which your right hand always wins the game?

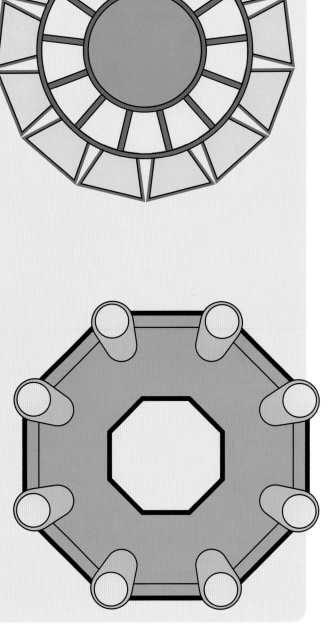

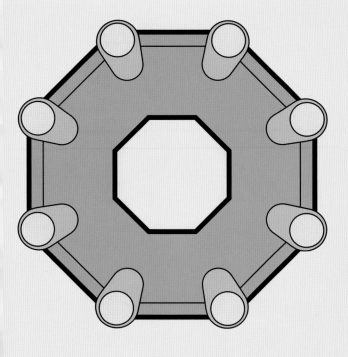

Gridlock

Getting across town by car can be a nightmare, not only because of the traffic but because the crazy road signs always seem to force you to go where you don't want to be! In the town of Gridlock, the problem is even worse: The town traffic authorities have increased the number of signposts, and have invented some new ones, so that at most crossroads there is at least one way you cannot turn. Getting from one side of town to the other now involves some surprising twists and turns.

ANSWER PAGE 104

Any direction ⊕		Ahead only →	
Ahead or right ⊢		Right only ↘	
Ahead or left ⊣		Left only ↗	
Left or right ⋎			

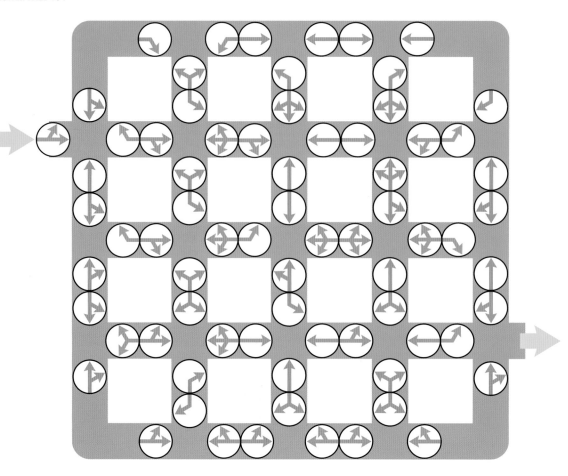

Can you find a route across town—beginning on the left and ending on the right—obeying the signs at each junction?

Crossroads

For this puzzle you need seven coins or counters. The challenge is to place all seven coins in sequence on seven of the eight circles.

But to do this every coin must first be placed on an empty circle and slid along one of the two associated lines to the circle where it will remain. The difficulty increases as you play: Can you continue to find empty circles so you can follow the rules and move coins where you want them?

ANSWER PAGE **104**

There is a simple strategy to complete the puzzle every time, no matter where you start. Can you work it out?

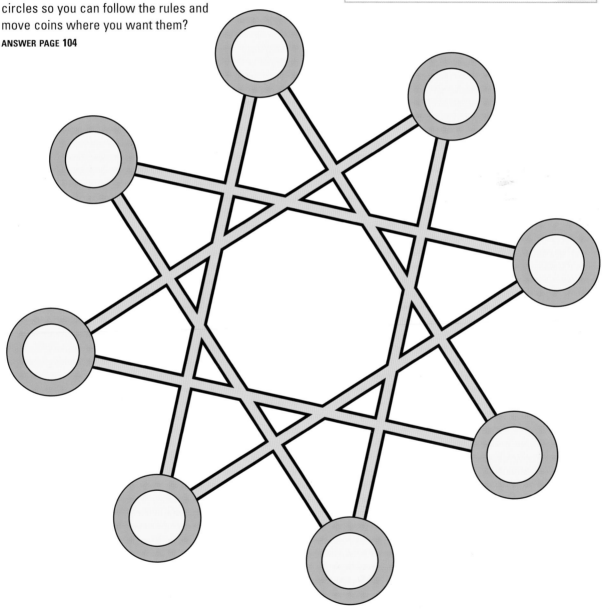

Separate and connect

The common theme behind the puzzles on these two pages is that of combination, either in linking or creating groups from the constituents of a linear collection.

ANSWERS PAGE 105

Cutting the necklace

Imagine you are a pearl fisher. Yesterday you dived and found only six pearls, which you put on a string, knowing that with just two cuts (as shown below) your partner, who makes up the pearl necklaces, could obtain groupings of any number of pearls up to the total six, as follows:

1 **by itself**
2 **as a pair**
3 **as a trio**
4 **as 3 + 1**
5 **as 3 + 2**
6 **as 3 + 2 + 1**

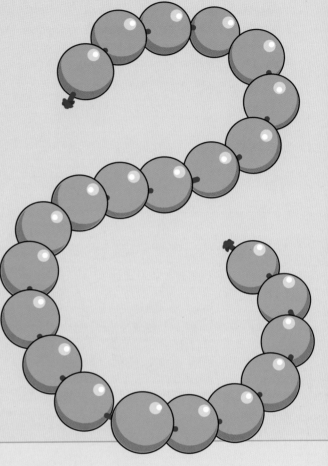

Today you have found 23. Where, in the string of 23, would you make four cuts in order to be able to obtain any number between 1 and 23?

Missing links

Below, in large figures, is an equation in which all the plus or minus signs have been left out. It is also possible that two of the numbers in the equation should have been printed together as a single number.

1 2 3 4 5 6

Factorial forty

It is possible to take just four numbers between 1 and 40 (inclusive) that singly or in different combinations, with a plus or minus sign placed between them, can total *every* number between 1 and 40. No number occurs more than once in any expression.

> *What are the four numbers? Can you fill in the table below with combinations of these four?*

	= 1		= 11		= 21		= 31
	= 2		= 12		= 22		= 32
	= 3		= 13		= 23		= 33
	= 4		= 14		= 24		= 34
	= 5		= 15		= 25		= 35
	= 6		= 16		= 26		= 36
	= 7		= 17		= 27		= 37
	= 8		= 18		= 28		= 38
	= 9		= 19		= 29		= 39
	= 10		= 20		= 30		= 40

The four numbers are:

> *Can you complete the sum so that it reads correctly? Two smaller number sequences are included to the right for you to use for practice.*

1 2 3 4 5 6 7 8 9 = 100

1 2 3 4 5 6 7 8 9 = 100

7 8 9 = 100

The Tower of Brahma

Many years ago, in India, I heard of a legend that a Hindu priest is steadily counting out the life span of the universe by moving the 64 disks that form the Tower of Brahma at a rate of one per second.

My game, involving four disks, will not take so long. It can be solved in only 15 moves. You need four disks of different sizes: Make your own or use four coins. Stack them up with the largest at the bottom and the smallest at the top. Assign a second and a third place that can be used for stacking.

ANSWERS PAGE 106

Shifting positions

The object of the game is to reproduce the original stack in the third stacking-place, using the second as a temporary transfer stage, as shown in the diagram below. Move only one disk at a time, and never allow a disk to rest on top of a *smaller* disk. The blank columns on page 37 are provided so you can draw in the disks to play the game. Alternatively, play out the game with coins or counters on the larger board at right.

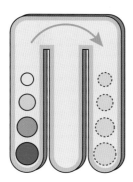

With four coins the transposition can be completed in 15 moves. How many moves does it take with only three coins?

The legend

An ancient Hindu holy man told me long ago that, in a certain great temple at Benares, there is a brass plate into which are fixed three pins. On one pin, at the beginning of time, there were 64 disks, the largest resting on the brass plate and the rest stacked up on top of it, in order of gradually decreasing size. Day and night, a priest transfers the disks from one pin to another at a rate of one per second, never allowing any disk to be placed on top of a smaller one, in order that one day the original tower will be rebuilt, all 64 disks in sequence, on one of the other two pins. That day will be the end of the world. How much time do we have?

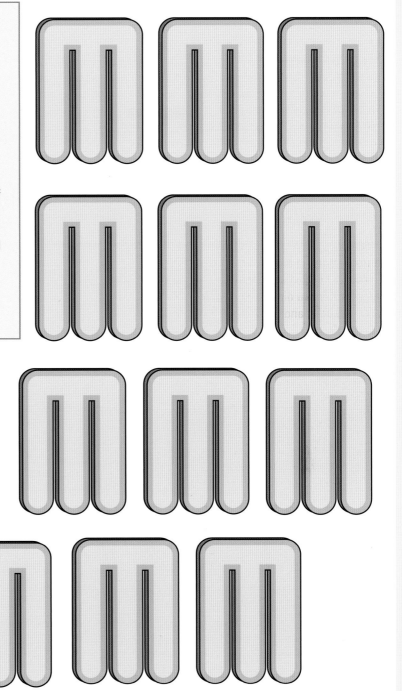

Interplanetary courier

My job as Interplanetary Courier at the Alpha Centauri spaceport means that I am responsible for transporting passengers from the spaceport up to the spaceliner circling in planetary orbit many zerks above us. And what passengers! In front of me stand a Rigellian, a Denebian, and an odd little creature called a Terrestrial. The shuttle craft can carry only two passengers at a time, and I am obliged to be one of them—but there are several nasty problems about that.

First, the Rigellians and the Denebians are officially at war: Left together by themselves in the airlock one of these two will be certain to suffer an unfortunate "accident." Then, unlike the vegetarian Rigellian, the Denebian is voraciously carnivorous: Left alone with the feeble Terrestrial for a second, there will very quickly be one fatter Denebian and no Terrestrial. Yet they all have to be ferried up to the liner's airlock, from which all three must pass into the care of the pretty reptilian hostesses.

ANSWER PAGE 106

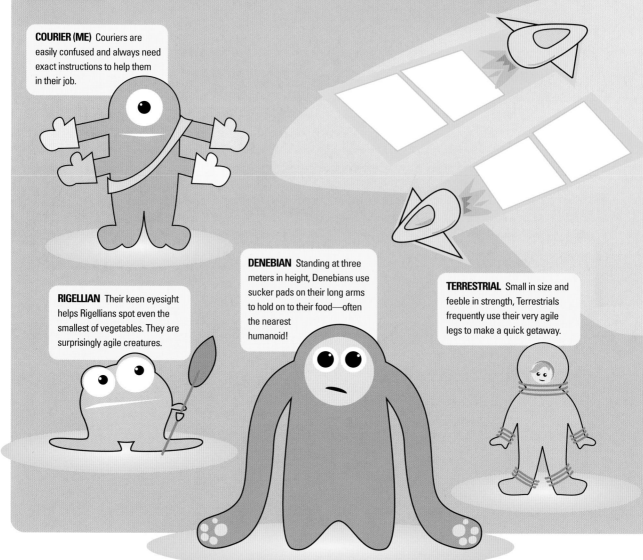

COURIER (ME) Couriers are easily confused and always need exact instructions to help them in their job.

RIGELLIAN Their keen eyesight helps Rigellians spot even the smallest of vegetables. They are surprisingly agile creatures.

DENEBIAN Standing at three meters in height, Denebians use sucker pads on their long arms to hold on to their food—often the nearest humanoid!

TERRESTRIAL Small in size and feeble in strength, Terrestrials frequently use their very agile legs to make a quick getaway.

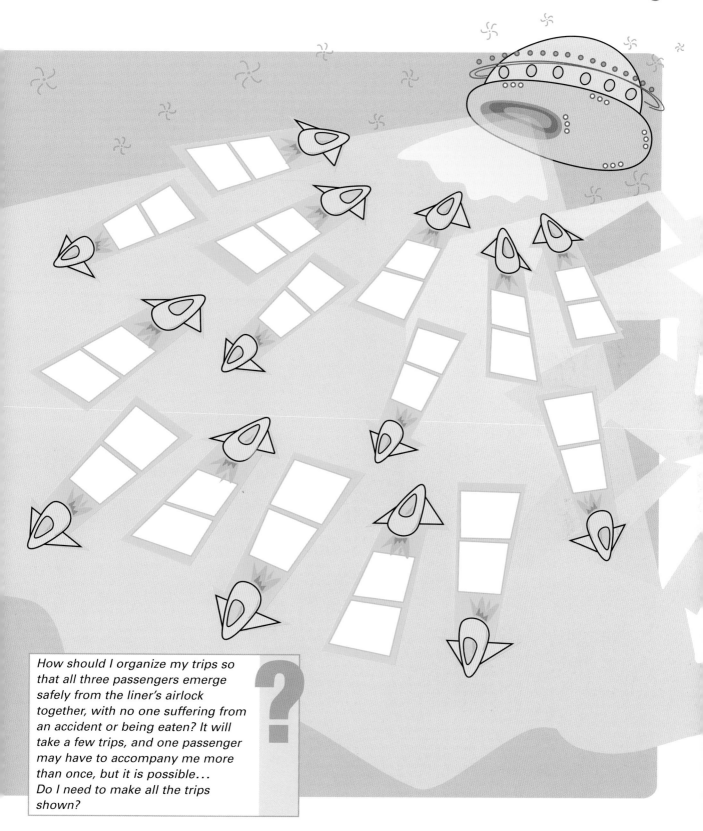

How should I organize my trips so that all three passengers emerge safely from the liner's airlock together, with no one suffering from an accident or being eaten? It will take a few trips, and one passenger may have to accompany me more than once, but it is possible... Do I need to make all the trips shown?

39

Husbands and wives

In days gone by, it was the convention that husbands would gallantly—and vigilantly—protect their vulnerable wives. So much so, that when three couples staying on an island together wanted to cross the surrounding water using a boat that could hold only two people at a time, a complicated scheme had first to be worked out to ensure that no wife was ever on the island or the mainland with a man who was not her own husband unless her husband was present too. She would be safe only in the presence of other women, or alone.

In consequence, the boat had to cross the water from or back to the island nine times in all, before the three couples were united again as a complete group on the mainland.

ANSWER PAGE 107

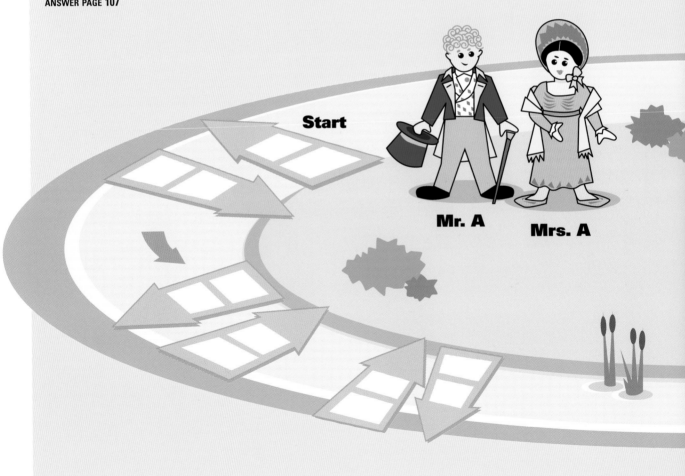

Start

Mr. A   Mrs. A

Can you work out which passenger or passengers the boat had to carry on each of the nine crossings? To make things easier, let's call the passengers Mr. and Mrs. A, Mr. and Mrs. B, and Mr. and Mrs. C.

Finish

Mr. C

Mrs. C

Mr. B

Mrs. B

41

The octopus handshake

Down, deep down among the coral reefs, where the fish frolic in the dim green depths, live two octopuses. They dwell in domestic bliss among the encrusted timbers of a sunken Spanish treasure ship. They have invented two games with nine pieces of eight they have found. One is simple and one more difficult.

ANSWERS PAGE 108

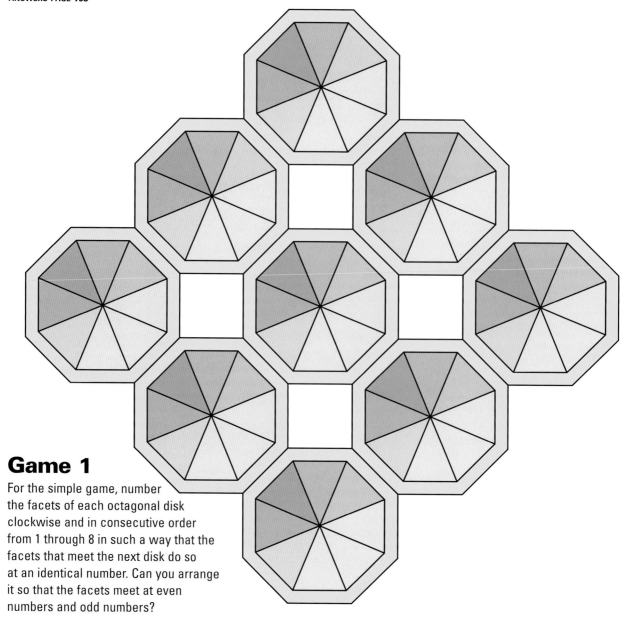

Game 1

For the simple game, number the facets of each octagonal disk clockwise and in consecutive order from 1 through 8 in such a way that the facets that meet the next disk do so at an identical number. Can you arrange it so that the facets meet at even numbers and odd numbers?

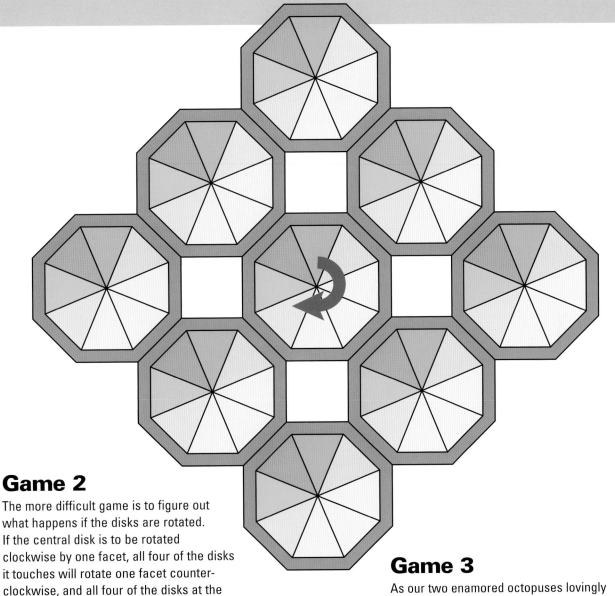

Game 2

The more difficult game is to figure out what happens if the disks are rotated. If the central disk is to be rotated clockwise by one facet, all four of the disks it touches will rotate one facet counterclockwise, and all four of the disks at the outer corners will rotate one facet clockwise (like the central disk).

Can you number the facets now so that *after the rotation* each facet that meets another disk will do so at an identical number?

Game 3

As our two enamored octopuses lovingly caress each other, they are very much aware that with eight tentacles each there are thousands of ways in which all eight of one could be in contact with all eight of the other. Can you calculate the total number of combinations, one-to-one, that are possible? How many are possible if each tentacle of one octopus touches each of the other only once?

Calculating the odds

If you're a gambler, you'll know that when you calculate odds it is very important to know the exact number of different possible outcomes. It is also valuable to know about any ways in which those outcomes can be usefully predicted.

ANSWERS PAGE 108

Pascal's triangle

Pascal's triangle can be used for several different types of calculation related to probability, or calculating the odds.

The pattern consists of an infinite arrangement of numbers in rows, each row having one more member than the one above it, and each internal number being the sum of the two numbers above it.

Suppose, for example, you were offered any two of four objects. The possible number of different combinations of two may be found on the triangle by reading along row 4 (ignore the top "1," so the row beginning 1, 4, 6…) and noting that the second figure along (after the initial 1, which must also be ignored) is 6. This shows that there are 6 possible combinations of any two of four.

If there is a chance element, the way to find out the chances of a specific two turning up from a total of four is to look at row 4 and compare the second along (6 again) with the total of all the numbers in the row. The result is a ratio of 6:16, or 3:8.

I have filled in the first few rows of the Pascal's Triangle for you. Can you complete the other rows as far as shown on this page?

Blaise Pascal

Blaise Pascal was a French mathematician and philosopher born in 1623. One of his many great contributions to math was his part in laying the foundations of probability theory, and it was during his research in this field that he made use of a special triangular pattern of numbers. The pattern can be traced back to the ancient Chinese—but is now generally called Pascal's triangle because of the ingenious applications he found for it.

Dicey problems

On this page there are two representations of the possible combinations resulting from throwing two dice.

One is a form of chart, showing the numerical totals made by combining the dice at the top and side of the grid.

The other shows the dice faces that go to make up those numerical totals, from 2 through 12.

Both prove that there are 36 possible combinations. Both also show that the combinations totaling 2 and 12 occur only once each among the possible 36—and the chances of throwing either are therefore 1:36. Finally, both also prove that the total 7 is the most common result, occurring six times in 36—and the chances of throwing such a combination is thus 6:36 or 1:6.

As noted above, because the possible total 7 can result from 6 different combinations out of 36, we say that that total has a 6:36—or 1:6—chance of occurring. Likewise the totals 2 and 12 have only a 1:36 chance of occurring.

Suppose you rolled two dice. Which totals have a 1:9 chance of occurring? Also, which totals have a 1:12 chance of occurring?

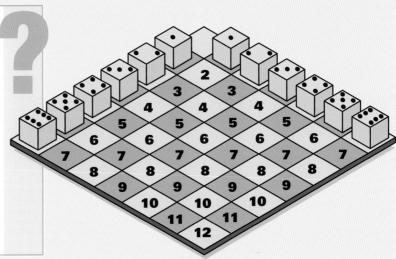

Gaussian curve

All the possible combinations of two dice are shown in dice faces, resulting in totals between 2 and 12. The columns in turn represent the "normal" or Gaussian curve—a graph that is fundamental to probability theory.

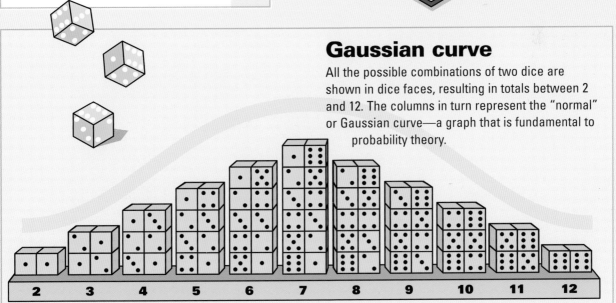

Up in the air

The puzzle on these pages explores all the possible outcomes if five small colored balls are tossed into five tubs. Every ball lands in a tub, but some may land in the same tub—there is room enough for all five to do so—and some tubs may remain empty.

Once you have found out all the possible combinations of balls in tubs—from a single ball in each tub to all five in one tub—you can get down to thinking about mathematical probabilities.

On these two pages we have provided 58 groups of five tubs. Try to work out all the possible distributions of the five balls that drop into them. It is fairly evident that there can be only one way of distributing all five balls in one tub; there is also only one way to put all five balls each in a separate tub—but what are the chances of either happening? You will need to know the total number of possibilities.

Use colored pencils to draw in the balls, or use numbers or letters to represent the different balls. (This shows that the puzzle can be solved mathematically too.)

ANSWERS PAGE 109

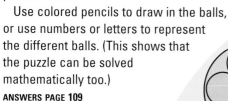

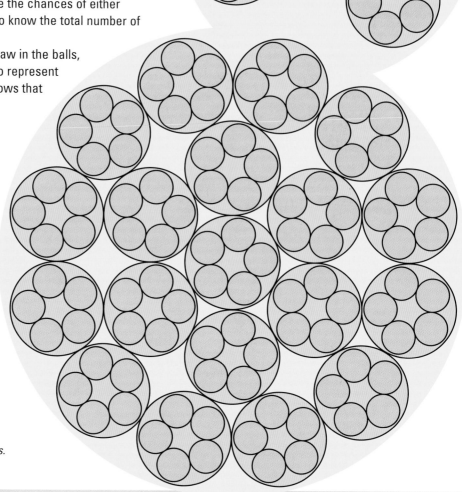

HINT *You will not need all of the tubs on these pages.*

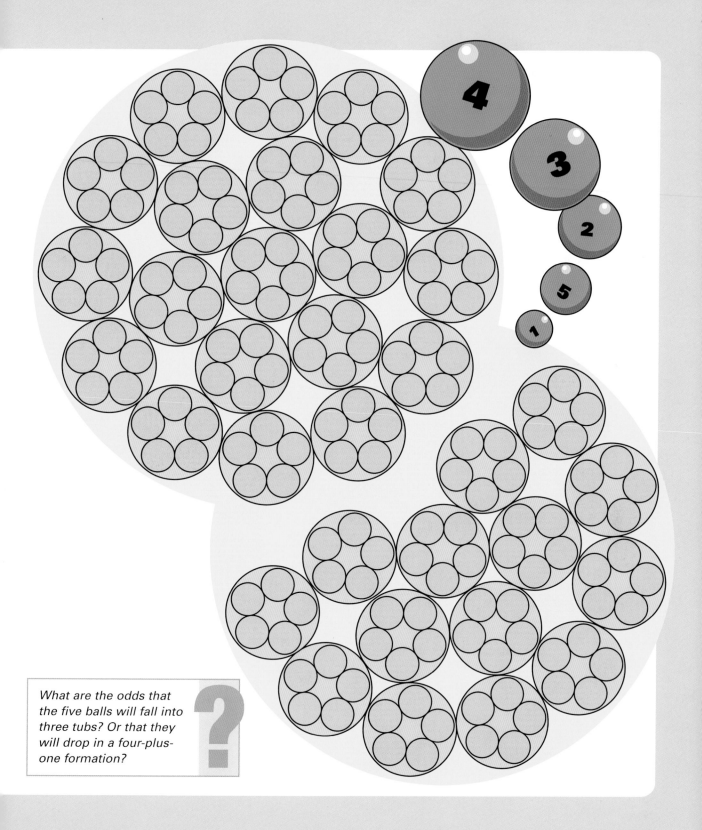

What are the odds that the five balls will fall into three tubs? Or that they will drop in a four-plus-one formation?

Lucky spinner, lucky dice

Here's some mathematical logic to do with transitivity. If object A is bigger than object B, which is bigger than object C, it follows that A must be bigger than C. Certain games appear to disobey this principle, however, and are thus said to exhibit "nontransitivity."

An example of one such game is the children's game of rock, paper, scissors, which has a circular winning arrangement: Scissors cut paper, paper wraps rock, and rock blunts scissors. Because paper beats rock and rock blunts scissors, if the game were transitive you would expect paper to beat scissors. This is not the case because it is nontransitive.

The games on these two pages are based on what happens when three do play this sort of game, and on the bias inherent in an apparently random chance of results.

ANSWERS PAGE 110

Game 1

The first game uses three spinners, which point to a value after being spun. The first spinner (A) has only one value: 3. The second spinner (B) is more complex; just over half of it (56%) has a value of 2, and just under half (the remaining 44%) is equally divided between values of 4 and 6. The third spinner (C) is divided so that just over half of it (51%) is worth 1 and the rest is worth 5. The game involves spinning the arrows to see which spinner beats which.

A

B

Which is the most successful spinner if there is to be a series of spins? Is it going to be any less successful, do you think, if there is to be only one spin of each spinner? Can you prove your answer mathematically either way?

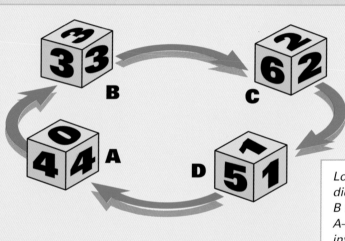

Game 2

Here we have a special set of four dice. Just how special can be seen from the "plans" of the six faces of each of them—A, B, C, and D. The set is carefully designed to demonstrate nontransitivity.

Looking at the numbers on each die, can you see why A beats B, B beats C, C beats D, and D beats A—and what is the probability involved?

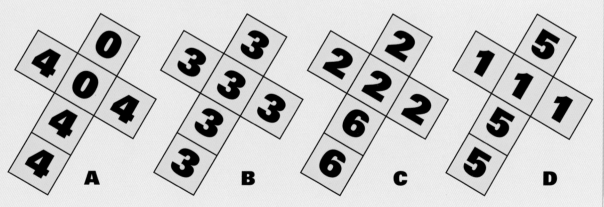

Hidden shapes

Shapes and patterns often disguise each other—this is part of the secret of camouflage. Here are six patterns and 12 shapes. Each pattern contains more than one shape. Can all the shapes be found? Can you discover which shapes are hiding in which patterns?

ANSWERS PAGE 111

HINT *The shapes you are looking for in the patterns are exactly the same size as the ones arranged around the outside.*

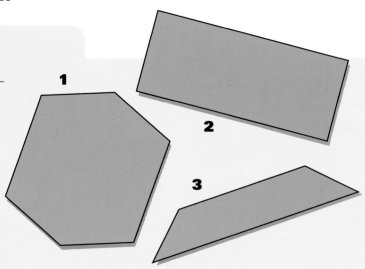

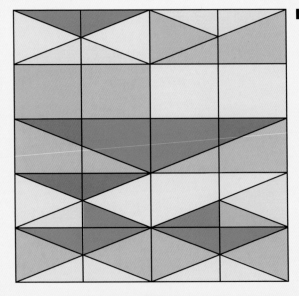

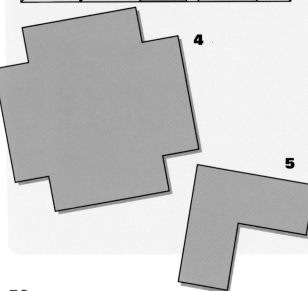

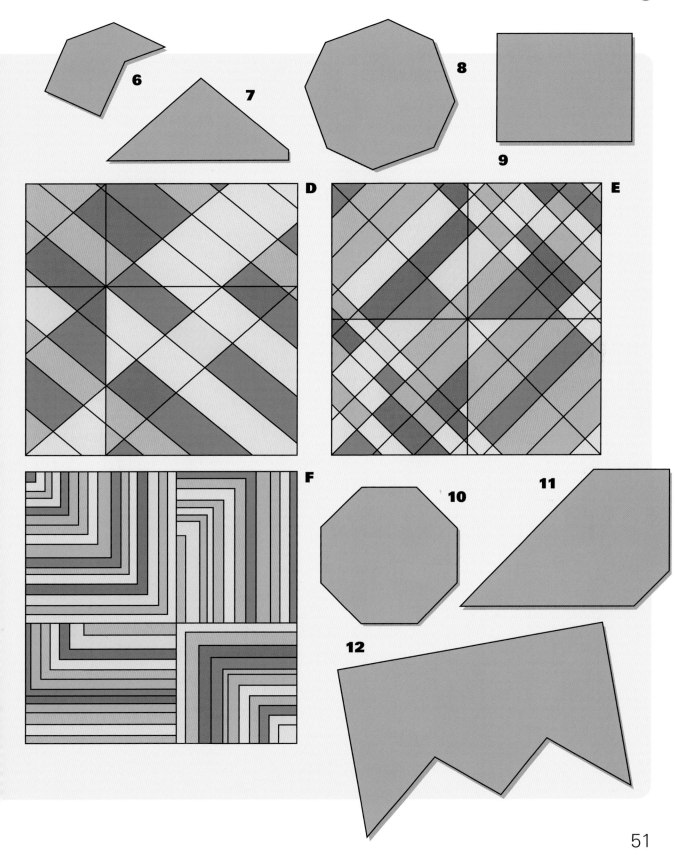

Match the lines

This puzzle contains a visual code created when the patterns of lines labeled 1 through 6 are combined with the patterns labeled A through G. To catch you out, I've deliberately combined 11 of the patterns incorrectly. Which are they?

ANSWER PAGE 112

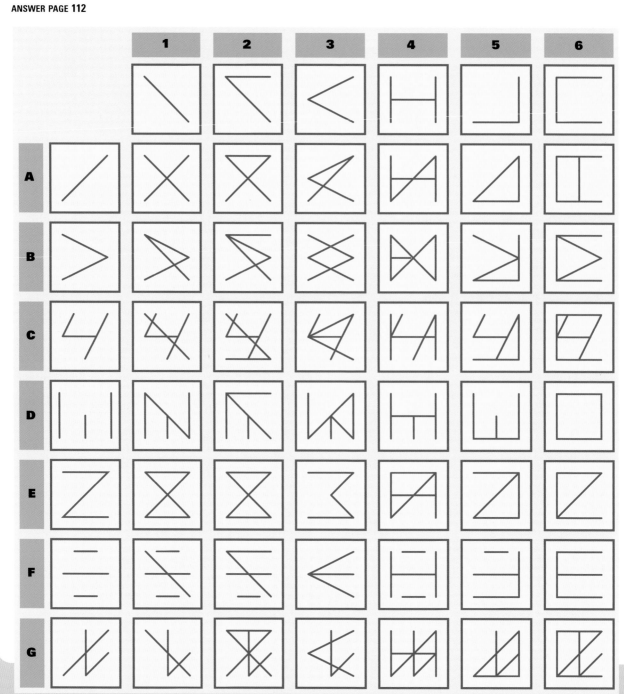

	Change 2 matches	Change 3 matches	Change 4 matches
Create 2 squares			
Create 3 squares			
Create 4 squares			
Create 5 squares			

Square the match

Matchstick games are always popular … but they're not always easy. These involve moving matches (or any movable short, straight objects of the same length) to create new patterns made up of squares.

ANSWERS PAGE 112

Moving only as many matches as directed, and creating as many squares as requested, can you complete these puzzles? (Squares may overlap or have corners in common.)

Tracks and traces

Michelangelo, the famous Italian painter and sculptor, is said to have been able to draw a perfect circle freehand. Don't panic—I'm not asking you to do that! But a circle is an excellent example of a continuous line that completes a pattern and returns to where it began. The puzzles on these pages run along similar lines.

To draw the envelope-shaped design on the right (shape 1) with an unbroken line, start at the bottom left corner and follow the arrows. You can trace the pattern in one continuous line. Unlike a circle, however, this line does not end where it started.

ANSWERS PAGE 113

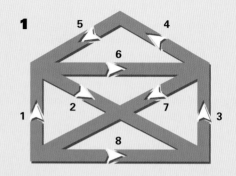

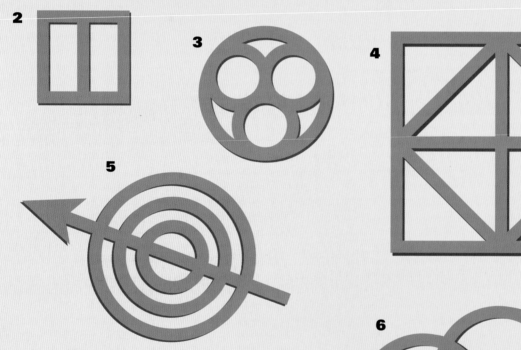

Can you trace designs 2–11 on these pages? In each one, put your pencil anywhere you wish to start, and see if you can complete the pattern without taking your pencil from the paper. Are there any in which you can make your line end where it started? Lines may cross but must not be retraced.

Impossible traces

Certain shapes, superficially similar to those I have challenged you to trace, are impossible. If you try to trace around a circle with a cross inside it, for example, you'll soon find yourself forced to duplicate a line—which breaks the rules of this puzzle. Some impossible traces have been included in the shapes presented here, just to make things *more* challenging. You may already have discovered which they are. But can you work out *why* they are impossible?

Count the cubes

"Putting things into perspective" is a common phrase. Perspective not only helps to bring three-dimensional realism to a two-dimensional representation, it also helps us to interpret things we can't actually see, because it creates certain visual rules. In the designs shown, there are various combinations of cubes stacked together. Most are simple heaps—but some require you to understand that one or more rows of cubes continue behind others, out of sight. This is an example of a problem involving spatial relationships, which is the particular object of this puzzle.

ANSWERS PAGE 114

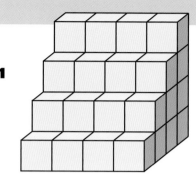

1

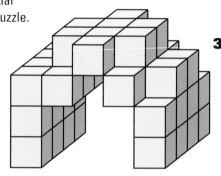

2

3

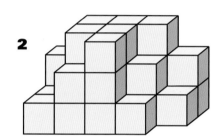

4

5

6

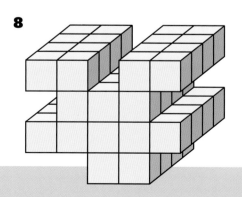

7

Game 1

Can you list the number of cubes in each stack, based on the visual evidence given, and with the further information that all rows of cubes are solid (complete) unless you can actually see them end?

8

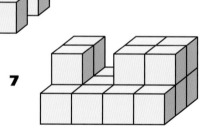

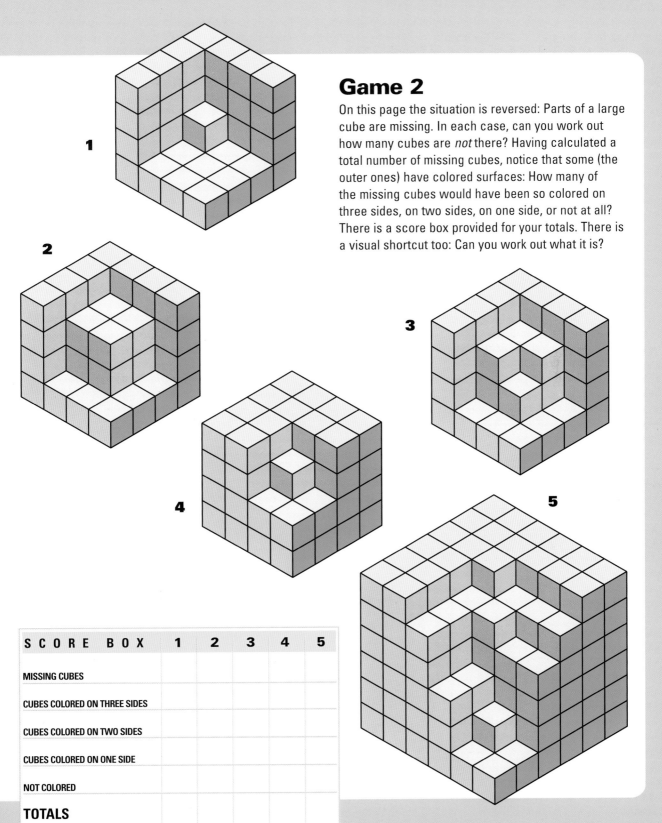

Game 2

On this page the situation is reversed: Parts of a large cube are missing. In each case, can you work out how many cubes are *not* there? Having calculated a total number of missing cubes, notice that some (the outer ones) have colored surfaces: How many of the missing cubes would have been so colored on three sides, on two sides, on one side, or not at all? There is a score box provided for your totals. There is a visual shortcut too: Can you work out what it is?

S C O R E B O X	1	2	3	4	5
MISSING CUBES					
CUBES COLORED ON THREE SIDES					
CUBES COLORED ON TWO SIDES					
CUBES COLORED ON ONE SIDE					
NOT COLORED					
TOTALS					

Dividing the square

Here's a popular type of puzzle that involves dividing a regular shape into different-shaped parts of equal area. Mathematically, we would describe these shapes as congruent, meaning you could rotate one half and match it exactly to the other half. Try this first with halves and then with quarters, below.

ANSWERS PAGE 115

Below and right are two series of squares with a 4 x 4 internal grid. In the first series (right), can you divide the squares into six different shapes, each being congruent halves, using the lines of the grid? In the second series (below), can you divide the series into five shapes comprising congruent quarters, using the lines of the grid?

Divide into halves

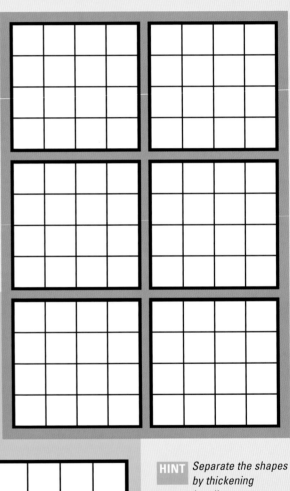

Divide into quarters

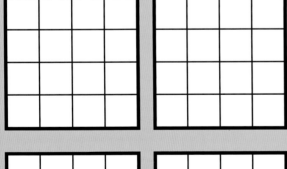

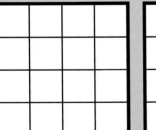

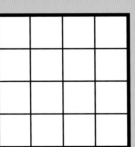

HINT *Separate the shapes by thickening appropriate lines to create obvious boundaries to congruent parts, rather than shading in the shapes, as this may lead to confusion.*

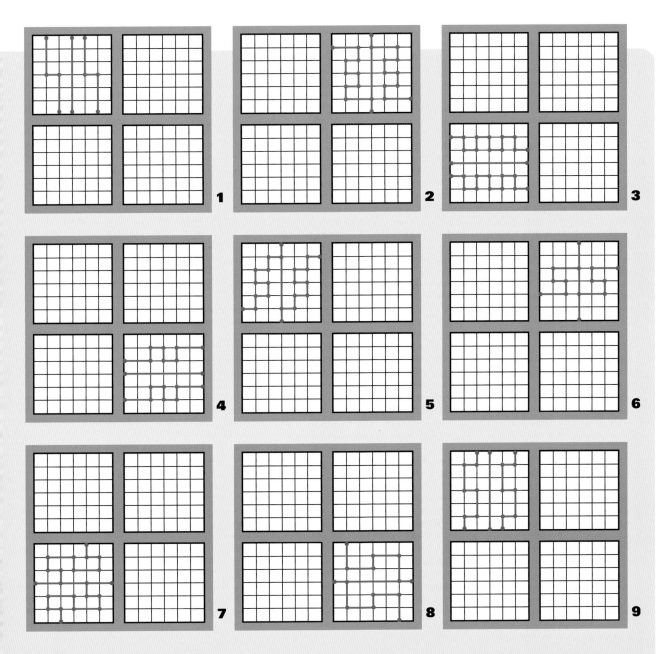

To solve the problem of quartering a square with a 6 x 6 internal grid is more difficult. Division can be based on two half-squares that are then halved again.

Can you divide the squares above into quarters of the same area and shape using the gridlines? One in each set of four has been done for you—can you do the other three? The problem is quite easy to solve once you have worked out the visual logic for grouping the squares into sets of four.

HINT *There are obvious equivalences in the ways that squares of a set of four are divided.*

59

Cube problems

A cube placed with one side on a surface can be turned around to face any of four directions without being turned over. That's four directions per side, and the cube has six sides—so the total number of ways a cube can be placed on a surface is 6 x 4, or 24.

ANSWERS PAGE 116

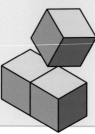

Game 1

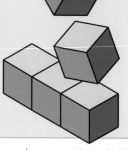

Game 2

If a cube can be placed on a table in any of 24 ways, in how many ways can two cubes be positioned side by side with one face of each touching one of the other?

When three cubes are placed side by side and kept in the same order, what is the total number of different ways the cubes can be turned, while keeping the same side-by-side arrangement?

Five of the six dice shown here represent different views of just a single die; each view reveals only three of its sides. However, some symbols on the dice are missing, and one of the views is deliberately misleading: It is from a completely different die.

Can you work out what the missing symbols should be, based on the sides that are pictured? You may find it helpful to plot the overall plan of the completed die, so I've provided an empty plan on the right for you to fill in. Which is the odd die out?

Game 4

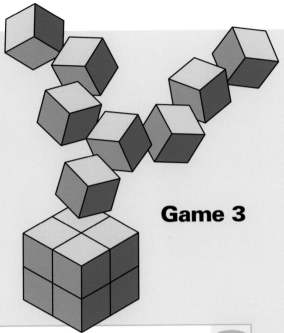

Game 3

Try again with eight cubes forming a larger cube. If the cubes remain in their present positions relative to each other but can turn every which way to touch those that are adjacent, what is the total number of ways individual cubes can be turned?

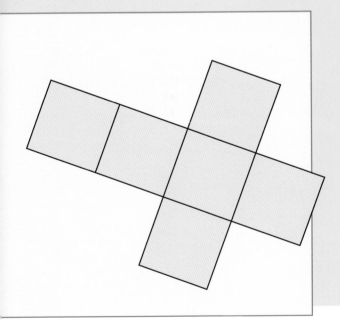

Pegboards

Pegboards are used in many games and educational activities. Almost all of them consist of squares divided into smaller squares: On this page I have represented the pegs or holes as dots, and the connectors between pegs as lines between dots. Some pegboards are arranged differently, but the same principles apply.

ANSWERS PAGE **117**

Game 1

In a 4 x 4 pegboard, how many different sizes of square can you create by connecting pegs? How many squares can you find all together?

HINT *Squares do not have to have horizontal bases.*

Game 2

In a pegboard consisting of two crossed parallel rows of holes, how many squares—of any size—can you create by connecting pegs? Corners of the squares must be at pegs.

Game 3

If the pegboard above has a peg in every hole, can you remove six pegs so that every square you found before now has no more than three corners marked with pegs, so that no squares of any size remain?

61

Inside-outside

As you know, the size of the inside of a shape depends on both the size *and* the shape of the perimeter. This can be demonstrated by taking a loop of cord and stretching it tightly between two points: A very thin strip is enclosed, with a small area. If the loop is made to form a circle, the area enclosed is considerably greater, although the perimeter—the length of the outside—has not changed.

If a pegboard has a band stretched around four pegs, enclosing an area (as shown below), can you calculate the area, in unit squares, enclosed, without measuring anything? The trick is to count the unit squares crossed by each length of band and to calculate the proportion of area enclosed.

For each *part* square within the perimeter band there is an equivalent shape of exactly the same size

somewhere outside the band: The result is that certain rectangles appear to be divided in half by the band, so the area of that rectangle on the *inner* side of the band is exactly half the total area of the rectangle. Use this principle to solve the problem. For practical purposes, assume that the band is simply a line with no thickness.

ANSWERS PAGE 118

The perimeters of all the figures below are identical in length. But how much area is enclosed (or covered) by each? And which has the largest area? Calculate the areas using the superimposed grid, in grid-square units, then fill in your answers.

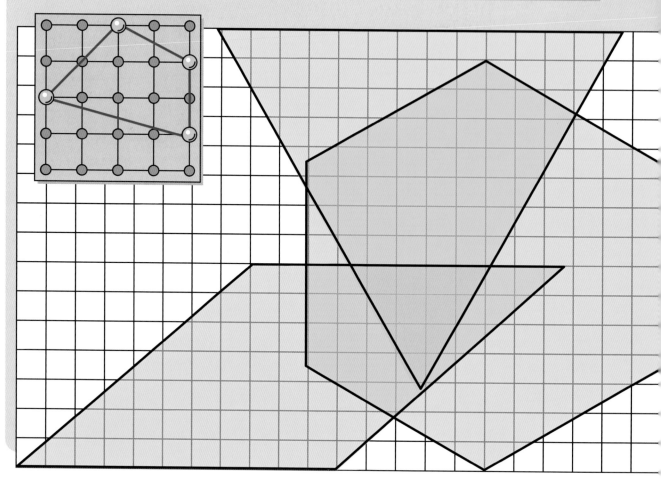

The island problem

The ancient Greeks knew all about the significance of the perimeter in terms of the area enclosed—indeed, the word "perimeter" derives from two Greek words meaning "measure around." Many Greeks lived on islands and had good reason to be aware of the pitfalls of area measurement. After all, it is easy to see that the area of an island cannot be assessed by the time it takes to walk around it: If the coastline is long, it does not necessarily mean that the island is large. Nevertheless, the 5th-century writer Proclus tells us that some landowners based real estate values on perimeter, not area.

An ancient story tells of Dido, legendary princess of Tyre, who fled to a certain spot in North Africa. Granted as much land there "as could be covered by the hide of an ox," she had the hide cut into thin strips and sewn together to make one long length. Then, using the shoreline as a natural boundary, she had her people stretch the hide cord out in as big a semicircle as possible, eventually enclosing an area of no less than 25 acres. It was this area that soon became the powerful and famous city of Carthage, scourge of the Romans.

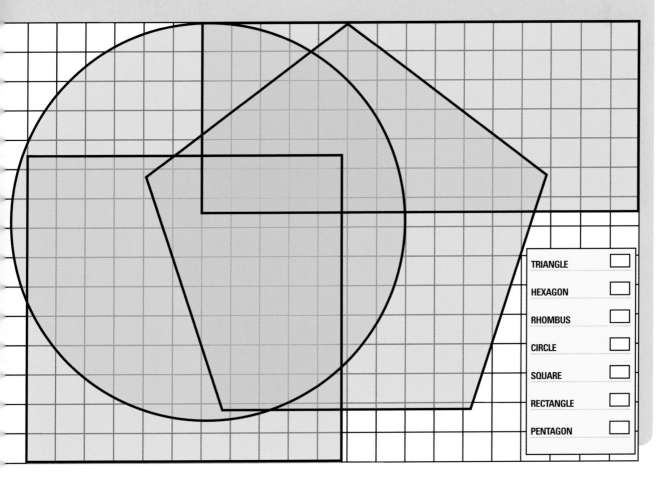

TRIANGLE	☐
HEXAGON	☐
RHOMBUS	☐
CIRCLE	☐
SQUARE	☐
RECTANGLE	☐
PENTAGON	☐

Repli-tiles 1

Did you know that some shapes, if they are combined with a specific number of identical shapes of the same size, create a larger version of themselves? And, correspondingly, when such shapes are subdivided appropriately they also make smaller versions of themselves?

Well, they do, and this is particularly evident with squares and equilateral triangles, as shown at right. It is also true of many other regular three- and four-sided geometrical figures (of which the rhombus and the isosceles triangle are examples).

Among other shapes that can be subdivided into miniatures (or mirror-image miniatures) of themselves are rectangles from which one quarter has been removed. Shown below is a square that has had one quarter removed and then has been subdivided into four equal internal miniature versions of itself.

ANSWERS PAGE 119

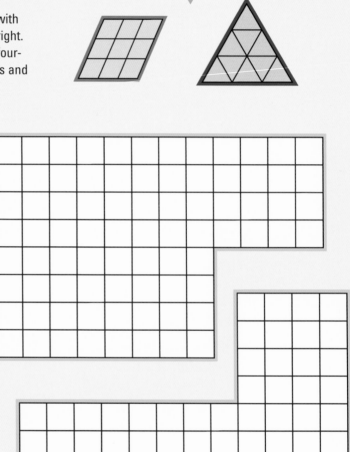

The same principles apply to the two large figures on this page. Can you subdivide them so that four miniatures can be created within each? A grid has been superimposed to help you.

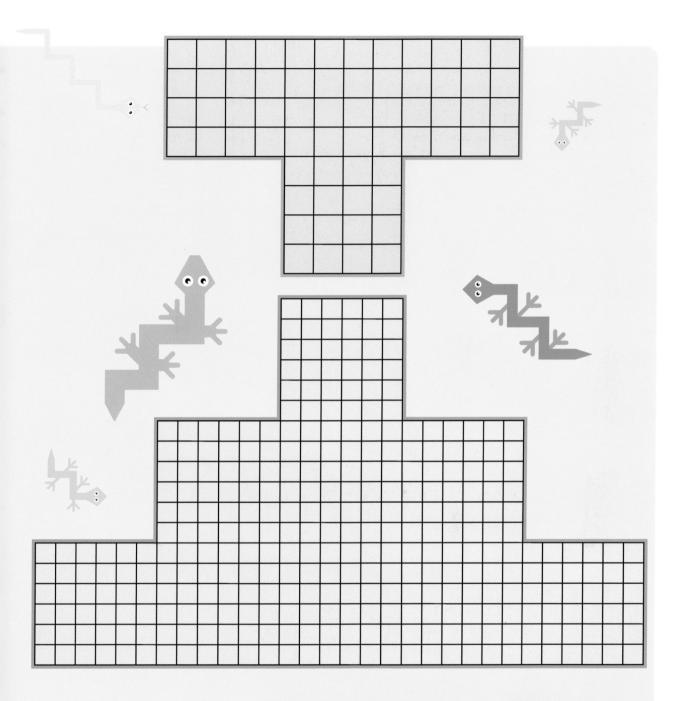

On this page are two further shapes that can be subdivided into miniatures of themselves. Can you work out how many shapes divide exactly into each larger shape?

?

HINT *The number of miniatures is likely to be much greater than you think.*

65

Repli-tiles 2

Here's another shape that can be subdivided into miniatures of itself—this time into small trapezoidal shapes, right, that (for the purposes of this puzzle, anyway) can be said to resemble a crab's shell. It's a shape that has no right angles, unlike the repli-tiles on the previous two pages.

ANSWERS PAGE 119

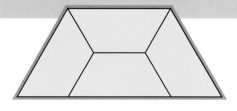

Game 1

On the beach, fishing nets are laid out to dry. One is a hexagonal crab net (right). How many crabs (see far right) will fit neatly into the net? Can you find two different patterns for arranging the crabs in the net?

Crabs

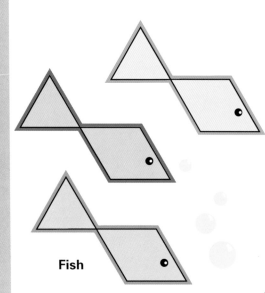

Fish

Game 2

Similar hexagonal nets (right) also catch fish. How many fish of the shape shown above can be caught in this net, if each fish retains its original shape?

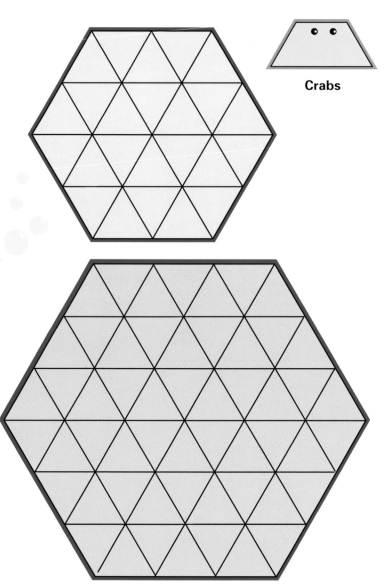

Game 3

Large fish also find these little ones delicious and, when they find a shoal, swallow as many as possible. If the small fish remain whole, how many can fit into the large fish?

On the rebound

The last pool ball is on the table: You have pocketed all the others and won the game easily. To celebrate, you plan to shoot that last ball from the bottom left-hand corner into a pocket to follow all the others—but you do not intend to shoot it directly. Your mastery of the game has to be demonstrated by pocketing the ball in as complex a way as possible, with at least two bounces off side cushions.

It is tricky to work out exactly where to aim the ball for its first bounce so that the identified pocket—the top left or the bottom right—is reached. It helps to imagine a grid superimposed over the table. The lines can be used as aiming markers at the edges of the table, and the squares can be used to judge that the angle at which the ball strikes a cushion is identical to that at which it rebounds.

ANSWERS PAGE 120

Game 1

You could use either of the courses shown below—but they are too easy, as they use only two side cushions. Instead, can you work out the path of a ball from the bottom left-hand corner:
Grid A to drop into the top left pocket;
Grid B to drop into the bottom right pocket, each time bouncing on at least three different cushions?

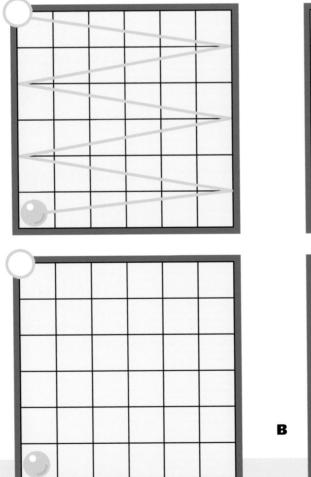

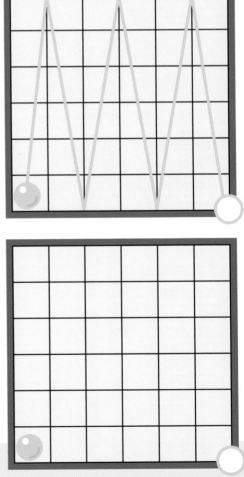

A

B

Game 2

Even on an L-shaped table, there is an easy way to pocket the ball top left or bottom right (shown on the two top tables), and a not-so-easy way. On the lower two grids, can you pocket the ball after bouncing it off at least four sides of the six, avoiding the central right angle, with:

Grid A five bounces before going off at the top left and, for extra effect,

Grid B seven bounces before going off at the bottom right?

HINT *You may have to calculate proportions within the squares of the grid.*

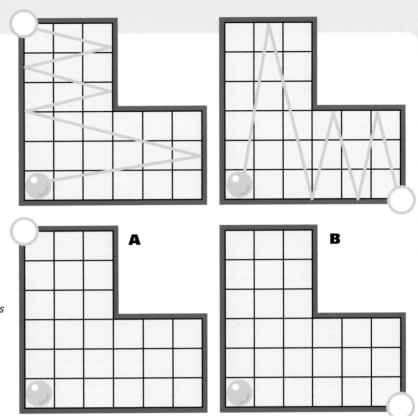

A

B

A

B

C

Game 3

If you found those easy, try your luck with even more irregular tables (left). With the ball starting bottom left, can you work out paths for the ball to be pocketed:

Grid A top left, after three bounces each on a different side;

Grid B top left of the right-hand section, after seven bounces;

Grid C bottom right, after 13 bounces on five different sides?

The ball may travel for as long as necessary. One of the three is in fact impossible. Which one?

HINT *Avoid both the central right angles in these shapes.*

69

A piece of cake

What could be easier than arranging the segments of these patterns so no two colored or numbered segments touch another of the same color or number? The more segments, the easier it is ... or is it the other way around? Either way, I'm sure you'll find this puzzle "a piece of cake."

The object is to color in the parts of the rings in the segments in such a way that the same color never touches itself, *even at a corner point*. I suggest you number the ring sections first (in pencil, which can be erased), then use a color for each number. There should be as many colors as there are rings in the cake.

For a three-segment, three-ring cake the object simply cannot be achieved with three colors. (So how many colors *are* required so that no one color touches itself even at a corner point, using as few as possible?)

The four-segment, four-ring cake can be colored according to the rules—but the final design is disappointingly symmetrical.

Is it necessarily so?

ANSWERS PAGE 121

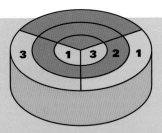

Impossible cake

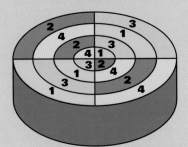

Possible cake

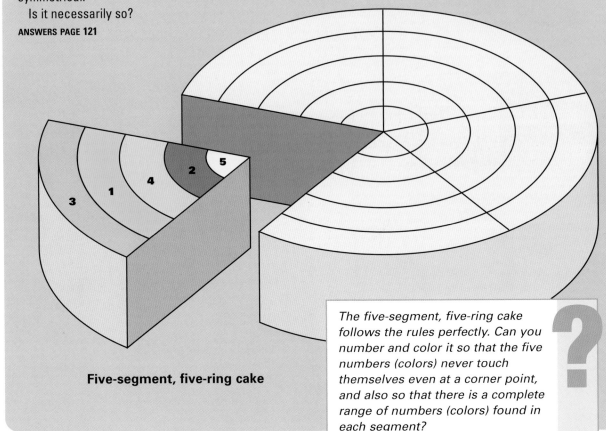

Five-segment, five-ring cake

The five-segment, five-ring cake follows the rules perfectly. Can you number and color it so that the five numbers (colors) never touch themselves even at a corner point, and also so that there is a complete range of numbers (colors) found in each segment?

Cake 1

The six-segment, six-ring cake also follows the rules. Can you complete it as you did for the five-segment cake opposite?

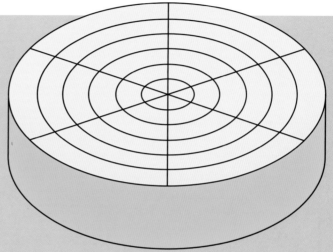

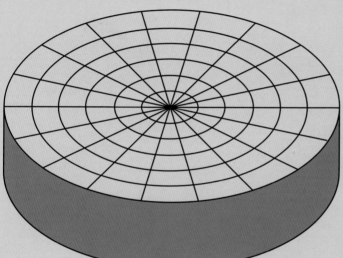

Cake 2

Here is a variation on the theme: an 18-segment, six-ring cake, probably big enough for my next birthday! Can you number or color it using only six numbers or colors?

It is a good idea to trace the design onto a separate sheet in case you make a mistake.

Cake 3

Finally, here is an 18-segment, five-ring cake. Can you do with it exactly what you were asked to do with the 18-segment, six-ring cake above, but using just five numbers or colors?

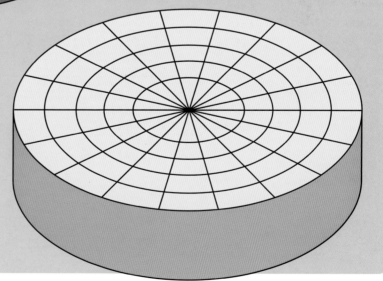

The hollow cube

Imagine you are peering into a hollow cube. At the bottom you can see a pattern of 6 x 6 squares. Another cube has a more regular pattern on an 8 x 8 grid. In both cases, only bits of the pattern can be seen at any time. But there is enough information in what you *can* see for you to construct or deduce the patterns, bit by bit.

ANSWERS PAGE 121

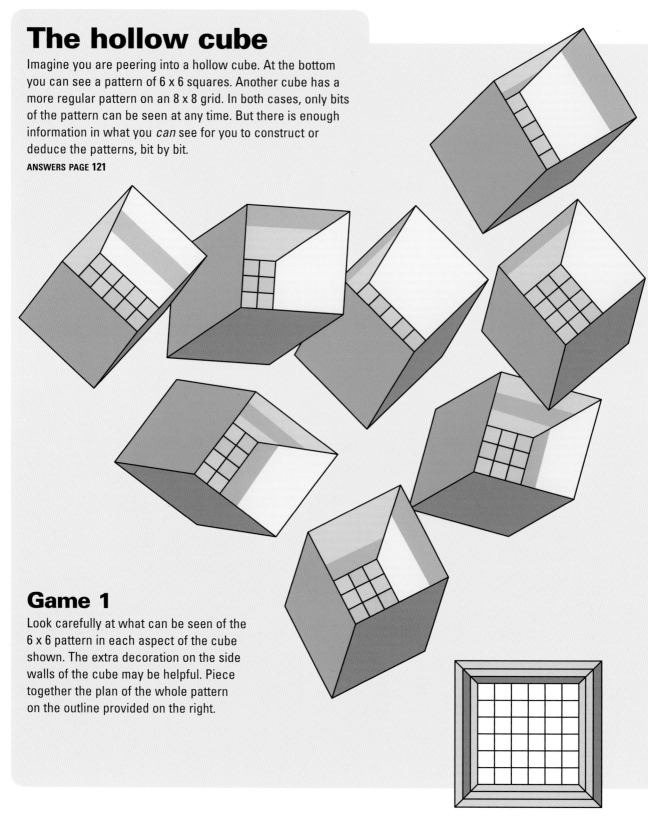

Game 1

Look carefully at what can be seen of the 6 x 6 pattern in each aspect of the cube shown. The extra decoration on the side walls of the cube may be helpful. Piece together the plan of the whole pattern on the outline provided on the right.

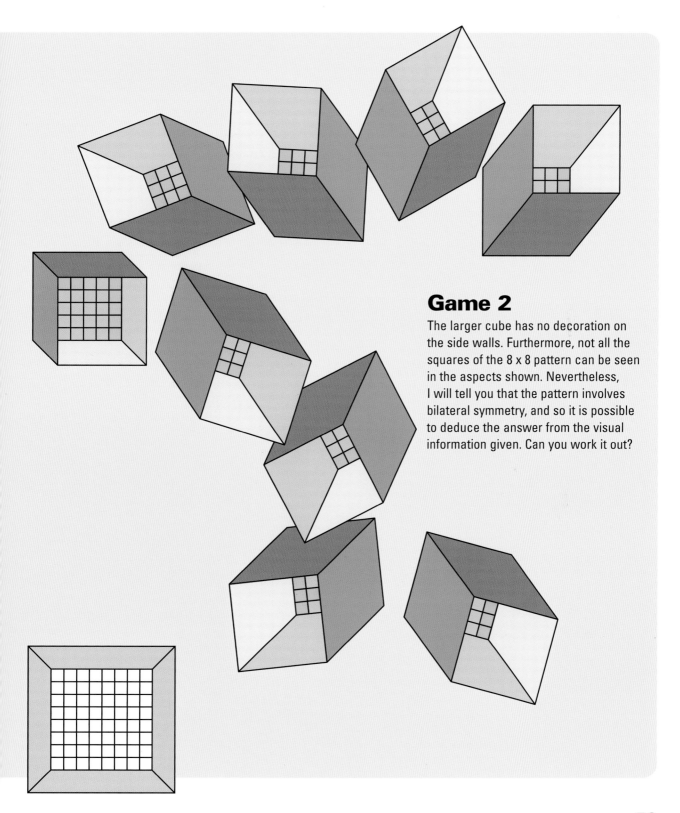

Game 2

The larger cube has no decoration on the side walls. Furthermore, not all the squares of the 8 x 8 pattern can be seen in the aspects shown. Nevertheless, I will tell you that the pattern involves bilateral symmetry, and so it is possible to deduce the answer from the visual information given. Can you work it out?

How many?

Each of the designs on this page contains a number of figures of the same shape—squares, triangles, or hexagons—in different sizes, some overlapping, some with common sides, some quite separate. Can you find them all?

ANSWERS PAGE 122

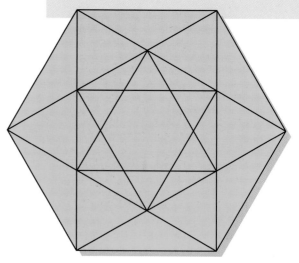

1 How many triangles?

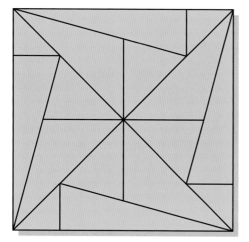

2 How many triangles?

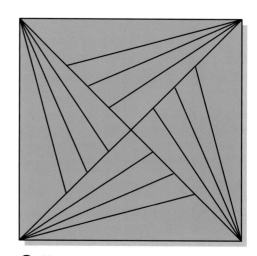

3 How many triangles?

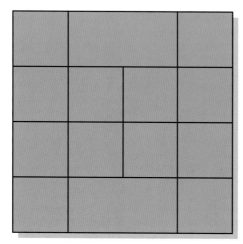

4 How many squares?

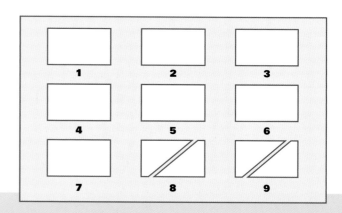

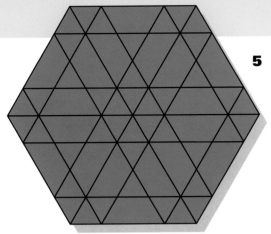

5 How many regular hexagons?

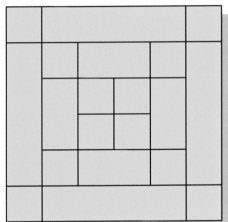

7 How many squares?

6 How many squares?

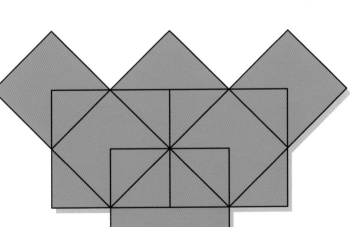

8 How many triangles and squares?

9 How many triangles and squares?

Cubes and routes

These strange shapes floating in space and the oddly made robot figure on the opposite page are designed to challenge your ability to think in three dimensions.

ANSWERS PAGE 122

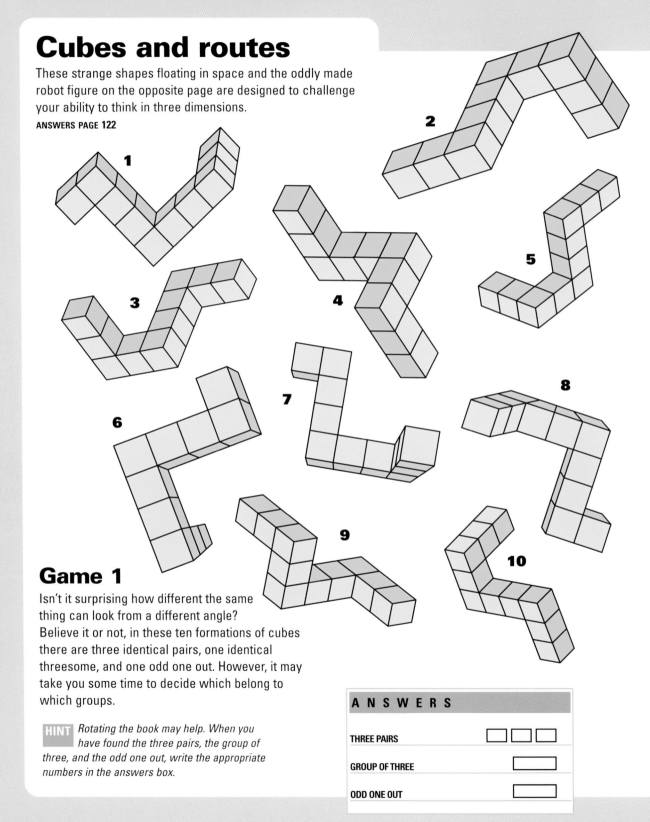

Game 1

Isn't it surprising how different the same thing can look from a different angle? Believe it or not, in these ten formations of cubes there are three identical pairs, one identical threesome, and one odd one out. However, it may take you some time to decide which belong to which groups.

HINT *Rotating the book may help. When you have found the three pairs, the group of three, and the odd one out, write the appropriate numbers in the answers box.*

ANSWERS			
THREE PAIRS	☐	☐	☐
GROUP OF THREE	☐		
ODD ONE OUT	☐		

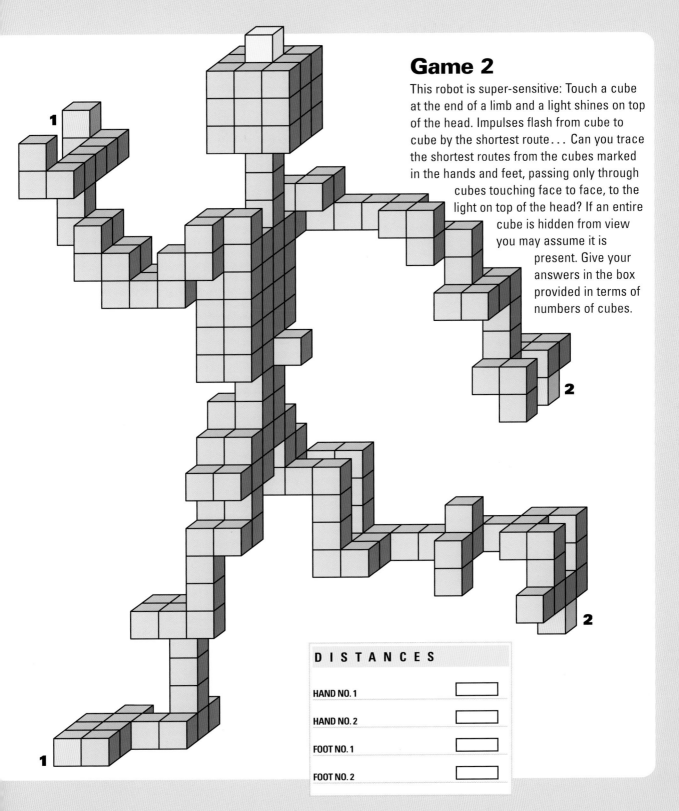

Game 2

This robot is super-sensitive: Touch a cube at the end of a limb and a light shines on top of the head. Impulses flash from cube to cube by the shortest route... Can you trace the shortest routes from the cubes marked in the hands and feet, passing only through cubes touching face to face, to the light on top of the head? If an entire cube is hidden from view you may assume it is present. Give your answers in the box provided in terms of numbers of cubes.

DISTANCES	
HAND NO. 1	
HAND NO. 2	
FOOT NO. 1	
FOOT NO. 2	

Find the polygons

At first glance the designs on these pages may seem no more than squares covered with crisscrossed lines, but look more closely. Can you spot regularities and symmetries: squares, triangles, rhombuses, kite shapes, and so on? You certainly should be able to, because this is the curious property of the design, which is remarkable for another reason too. The whole pattern is actually made up of four equilateral triangles of the largest size possible within the square, with one point in each of the square's corners.

ANSWERS PAGE 123

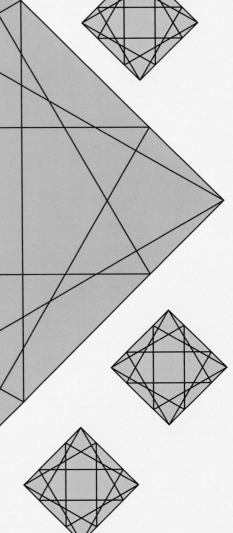

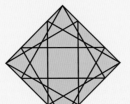

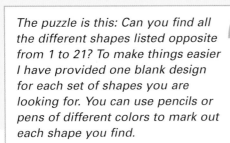

The puzzle is this: Can you find all the different shapes listed opposite from 1 to 21? To make things easier I have provided one blank design for each set of shapes you are looking for. You can use pencils or pens of different colors to mark out each shape you find.

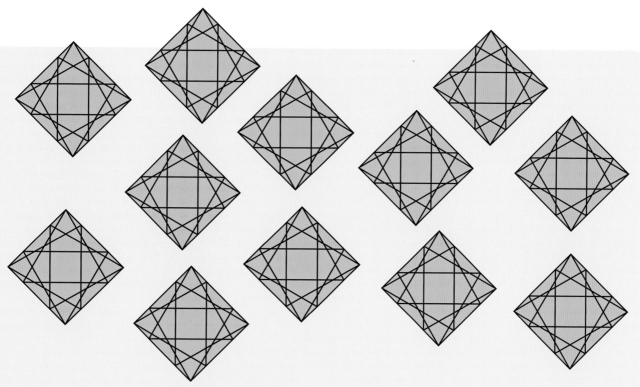

1 First find the 4 large equilateral triangles (triangles with 3 sides of equal length) that create the pattern in each square.

2 Then find 4 squares, not necessarily all of the same size.

3 Find 4 equal medium-sized equilateral triangles.

4 Find 8 equal small equilateral triangles.

5 Find 4 equal halves of a regular hexagon (shapes with 6 sides of equal length).

6 Find 2 equal large but irregular 6-sided shapes.

7 Find 2 equal medium-sized irregular 6-sided shapes.

8 Find 2 equal smaller irregular 6-sided shapes.

9 Find 1 irregular 8-sided shape.

10 Find 4 equal large right-angled isosceles triangles. (That is, triangles with 2 sides of equal length and a right angle between them.)

11 Find 4 equal medium-sized right-angled isosceles triangles.

12 Find 8 large right-angled triangles that do not have sides of equal length.

13 Find 8 medium-sized right-angled triangles that do not have sides of equal length.

14 Find the 8 smallest right-angled triangles that do not have sides of equal length.

15 Find 2 equal large rhombuses (figures with 4 equal sides that have both pairs of sides parallel).

16 Find 4 large parallelograms (figures with 4 sides that have both pairs of opposite sides parallel).

17 Find 4 medium-sized parallelograms.

18 Find 4 equal 5-sided shapes that overlap to form the outline of the irregular 8-sided figure found previously (**9**).

19 Find the 4 largest kite shapes (shapes symmetrical about the longest axis).

20 Find the 4 smallest 4-sided kite shapes.

21 How many *different* right-angled triangles can you find all together?

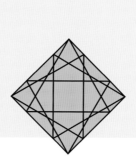
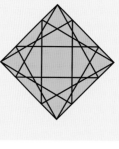

Multi-views

As your helicopter gently descends past a building to the ground, what do you see of the building? From high up you see only the roof laid out below you. Then as you sweep down and to one side, there is a completely different view. Yet it is the same building. The puzzles on these pages involve combining such differing viewpoints.

ANSWERS PAGE **123**

Overhead view

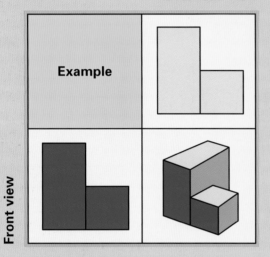

Example

Front view

Can you match the overhead view and the view from ground level with the three-dimensional view? Here are 16 structures—but from overhead it seems there are only four different views, and from the front at ground level there are again only four views. Combining the overhead and the front views, however, makes each of the 16 identifiable. Write your answers in the boxes provided.

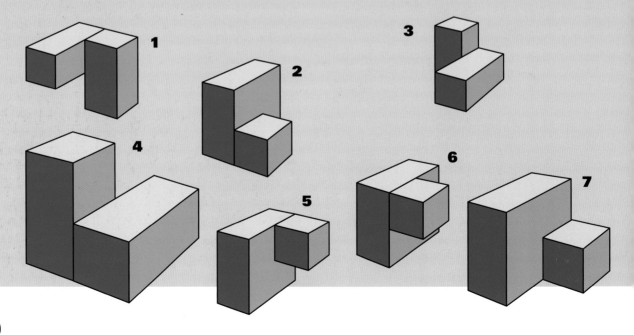

1
2
3
4
5
6
7

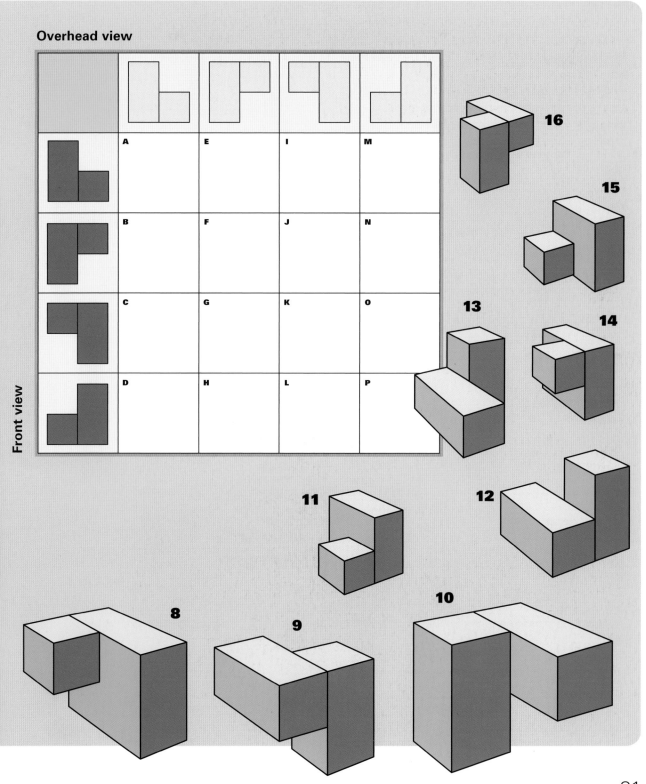

81

Distortrix 1

Have you ever looked at yourself in the distorting mirrors you find at the fair? Their surfaces are curved instead of flat, so that parts of the image are enlarged, and other parts are made smaller.

If you imagine a face to be made up of small square patches, as if you are looking at it through wire netting, a distorting mirror reduces some areas in comparison with others, enlarges some, and distorts many in different ways. On these and the next two pages are some distortions even stranger than those in fairground mirrors.

ANSWERS PAGE 124

On the right is the basic design, which you should transfer, square by square, to the distorted grids on the opposite page. Copy the part of the original outline in each original square onto the equivalent distorted "square" in the distorted grid. Shape 1 is an example to get you started.

Master shape

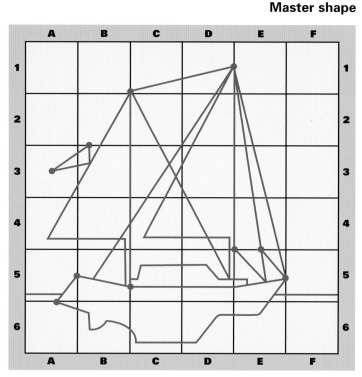

Shape 1

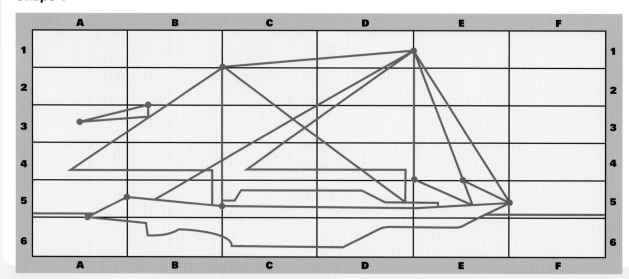

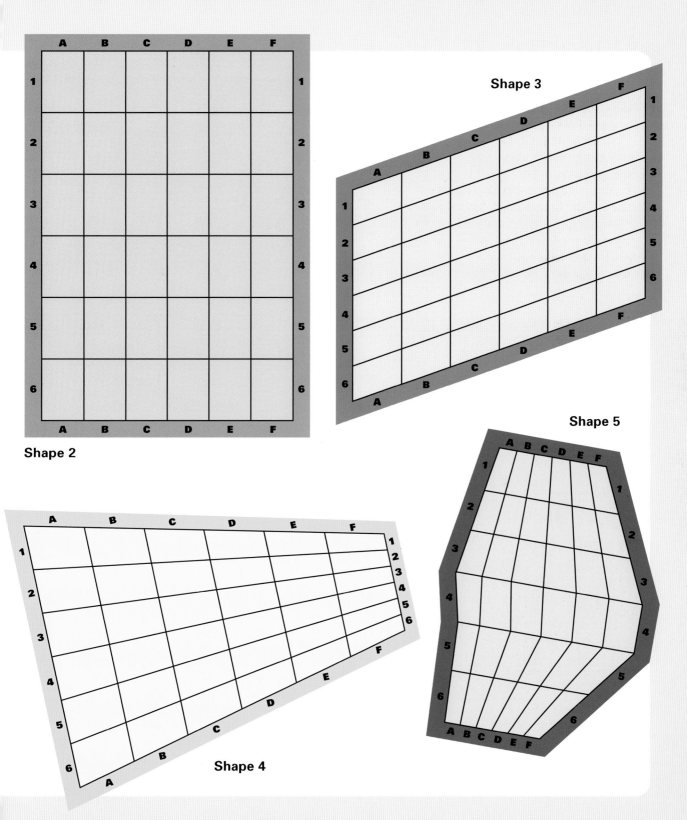

Shape 3

Shape 2

Shape 5

Shape 4

Distortrix 2

On these pages there are two distorted designs for you to decode using the normal grid. On the facing page, decode the pattern from the near-circular grid on to the straightforward square grid. What do you find?

ANSWERS PAGE 124

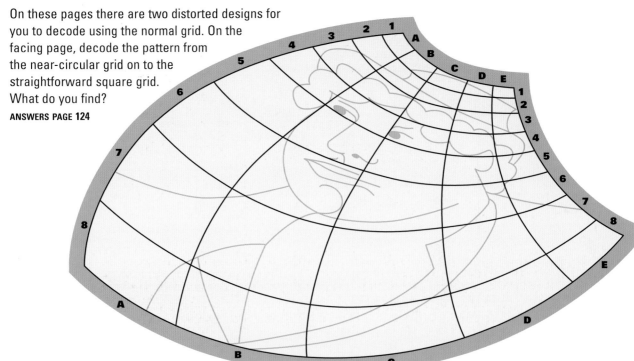

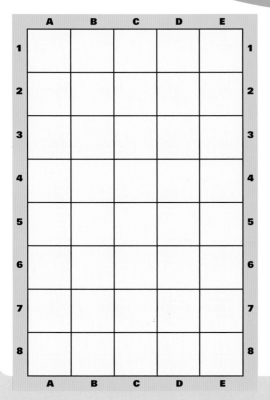

Anamorphic art

Distorted images have always appealed to those who like hidden meanings, or secret symbols. Sometimes people have found it necessary to create such images for their protection, not just for fun. In England during the reigns of kings George I and George II, for instance, supporters of the outlawed and exiled pretender to the throne, Charles Edward Stuart, would have been imprisoned for treason if they had been found with a portrait of their preferred monarch, the "King over the water." By means of distorted portraits, however, which came to life when viewed from a certain angle or through a curved mirror, they were able to conceal their allegiance. This technique is called anamorphic painting or art, and such works of art fascinate us even today.

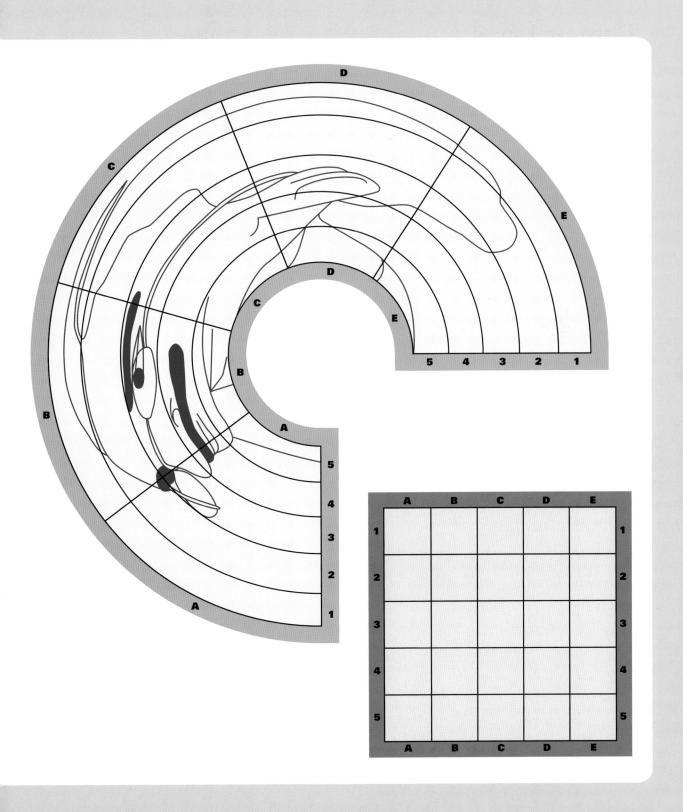

Space filler

See if you can divide the large equilateral triangle on this page and the parallelogram on the opposite page into as few smaller equilateral triangles as possible, using the lines of the grid, so that all the space is filled. This is not quite as easy as it at first seems, as you will see from the explanation below.

ANSWERS PAGE 125

Game 1

Following the rules explained below, what is the smallest number of equilateral triangles into which you can divide this large triangle containing 11 grid triangles per side?

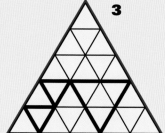

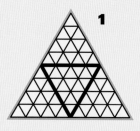

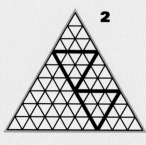

*Subdivision is quite easy when there are even numbers of grid triangles on each side (as in **1** above right). When there is an odd number of grid triangles, however, things are rather different. After the first division, you will find there is space left over; following the rules, this also has to be divided into as few equilateral triangles as possible. In a triangle in which the number of grid triangles per side is divisible by three, the method shown in example **2** is the most economic.*

*By a similar process, if the number of grid triangles per side is divisible by five, the method shown in example **3** is the most economic.*

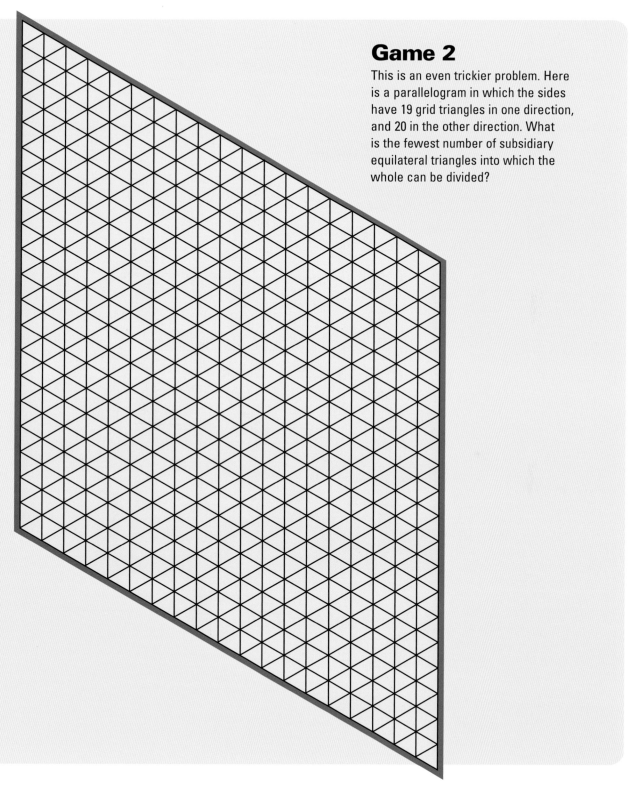

Game 2

This is an even trickier problem. Here is a parallelogram in which the sides have 19 grid triangles in one direction, and 20 in the other direction. What is the fewest number of subsidiary equilateral triangles into which the whole can be divided?

Subways

The subway is meant to be a quick way across town—and for many journeys it is. But in towns where there are more than two subway lines (indicated by different colors on the map) and just a few interconnecting stations, travelers have to get used to waiting around. And they also have to get used to time spent walking between platforms. On many subway systems, having to change trains is the equivalent in time of at least one more stop on the first train. And that is the statistic at the heart of the puzzles on these two pages.

ANSWER PAGES 125–126

Game 1

The object of this puzzle is to find the shortest route between specified stations (below), counting each station you pass (including the station at which you start) as 1 unit of time (or, therefore, effective distance), and any station (yellow cube) where you change lines as 2 units.

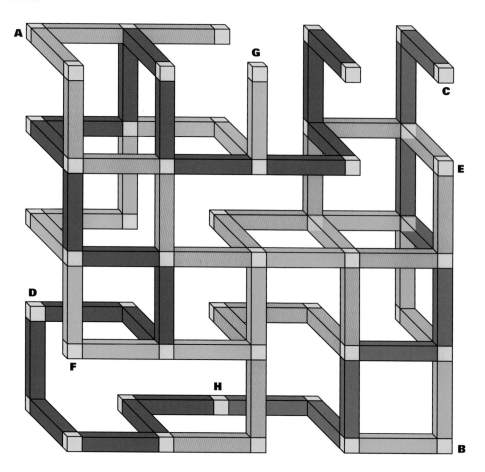

FIND	THE	SHORTEST	ROUTES	
A TO B			E TO F	
C TO D			G TO H	

Game 2

This puzzle is slightly more complex. Like the one on the previous page, however, this subway runs on two principal levels (representing a sort of three-dimensional cubic layout), but this time there is another line between the two, connected only at certain stations. This is the express line: There are fewer stations and so trains travel faster. The snag is: There are also fewer trains. In addition, the routes have been drawn at a more acute angle, so it is more difficult to be sure where you are going to end up.

FIND THE SHORTEST ROUTES			
A TO B		B TO C	
C TO D		D TO E	

The object is to find the shortest route between specified stations (above), counting each station you pass (including the station you start at) as 1 unit, any station where you change routes at 2 units, and each time you get on or get off the express line as 3 units (if you start at an express station, count the station as 1 unit.)

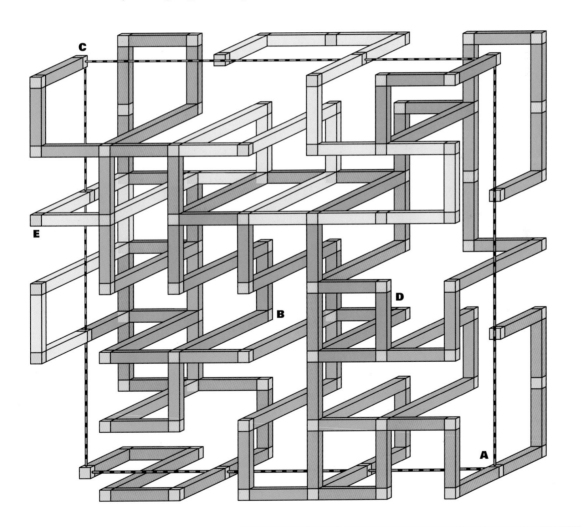

Computer patterns

The universe we inhabit is vast and the laws of nature are complex. Even a simple self-contained system or universe with simple laws can still hold many suprises.

Modern computers operate like small universes: The programs that control what they do are their "laws of nature." Even a simple progressive program can produce a rich variety of results.

ANSWER PAGES 126–127

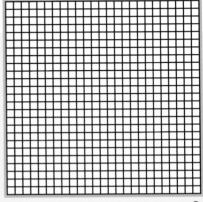

3

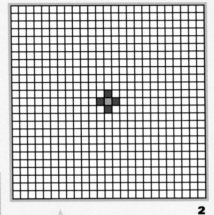

2

Start

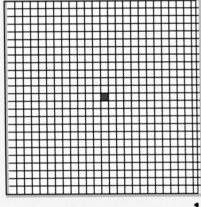

1

The computer pattern on these pages grows and becomes more complex following a small set of rules constantly applied. I have begun the progression for you, and put in a few later stages. Can you take it up from where I have left off, filling in the missing stages and successfully reaching the eleventh stage?

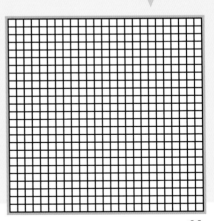

11

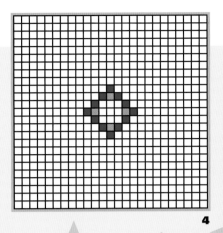

4

5

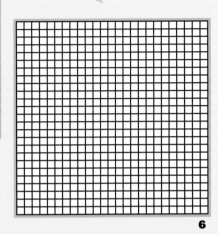

6

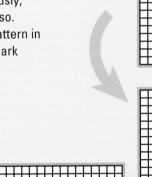

7

Rules

1 Dark green squares (or cells) survive for one stage of the pattern growth sequence, then change to pale green cells for the next stage. In the third stage, these pale green cells disappear and the cell becomes blank.

2 All changes occur simultaneously and instantaneously; and all cells that can change or be added *must* do so.

3 New (dark green) cells are added to the existing pattern in all blank cells that touch one side only of existing dark green or pale green cells.

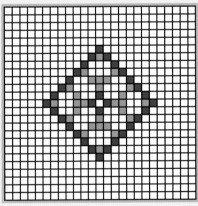

8

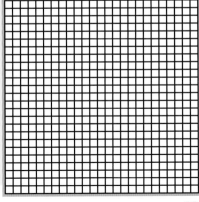

10

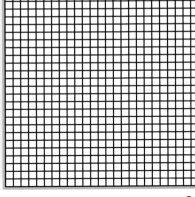

9

The answers

Finding the answer is only half the battle when it comes to puzzling. To expand your mind, you need to understand the reasoning behind the answer too. That's why this is an answer section with a difference. Not only do we talk you through the thought processes that go into solving the puzzles, so that next time you'll be quicker and get more satisfaction from completing similar puzzles, but we also fill you in on some of the fascinating historical facts about puzzles and numbers. We hope you'll find the answer section as absorbing as the puzzles themselves!

Match blocks PAGES 8–9

There are several possible solutions to both games. The ones presented here are among the most obvious.

Game 1

7	6	5	4	3	2	1
1	7	6	5	4	3	2
2	1	7	6	5	4	3
3	2	1	7	6	5	4
4	3	2	1	7	6	5
5	4	3	2	1	7	6
6	5	4	3	2	1	7

Game 2

7	5	3	1	6	4	2
1	6	4	2	7	5	3
2	7	5	3	1	6	4
3	1	6	4	2	7	5
4	2	7	5	3	1	6
5	3	1	6	4	2	7
6	4	2	7	5	3	1

About Match blocks

Match blocks in these same combinations can also be arranged to form a magic square (see page 16), in which all rows, columns, and diagonals add up to the same number. In fact, the solutions to these puzzles fulfill all the requirements of magic squares— inevitably so, because the numbers 1 through 7 are being arranged specifically to fall in each direction only once. The number each row/column/ diagonal adds up to is thus the total sum of the numbers 1 through 7 … which is 28. These match block puzzles were inspired by a special category of magic squares discovered by the Swiss mathematician Leonhard Euler and named by him Latin squares.

Finding the key PAGES 10–11

Key to the keys

You can do it with only two different key tops, with seven of one shape and three of another. Arrange the three so that two are separated from the third by one original shape, so that you can identify both the starting point (one different top) and the direction (two different tops together) in which to count the memorized sequence.

Combination lock

There are three repeated letters to be found. The secret code word is: MINDBENDER.

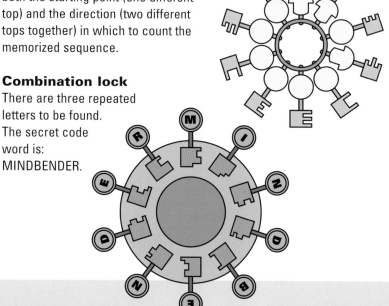

About Key to the keys

As with several other problems in this book, this puzzle is most easily solved by choosing a place on the circle from which to start, and by considering the keys to form a straight line from there. In other words, the puzzle can be simplified by looking at it in linear—as opposed to circular—terms. This is an important principle, although in all such cases it is also essential to remember that one end of your "line" is in fact contiguous with the other.

Continuous paths PAGES 12–13

The starting node for the sample game and Game A is the only one possible—because all arrows lead away from it, so unless you start there, that node will never be reached. Similarly, there is only one node from which Game B can start. Game B can end only at node 19 shown, because all arrows point to it and none points away. Multiple solutions to all of the puzzles exist, however.

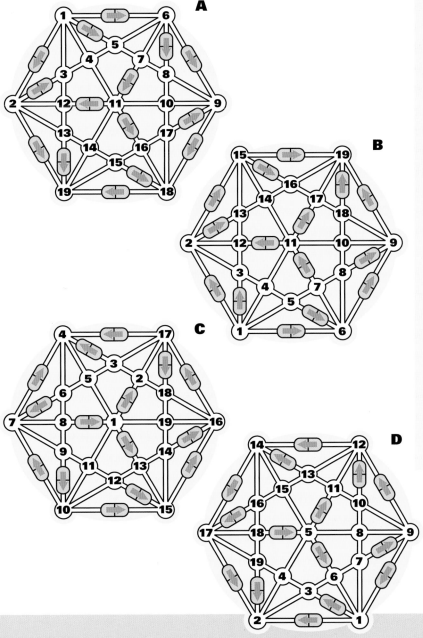

About Continuous paths

This puzzle is based on a far more complex version first presented by Sir William Rowan Hamilton in 1857 as a problem for scientists to work out mathematically. An Irishman, Hamilton was born in Dublin in 1805. He was very quickly renowned as a prodigy, being able to read English at the age of three, Latin, Greek, and Hebrew by the age of five, and Arabic and Sanskrit by the time he was ten. Two years later he read Isaac Newton's *Arithmetica Universalis*—and was hooked on math for the rest of his life. In 1822 he found an error in the work of the eminent French mathematician-astronomer Pierre-Simon Laplace (whose major and authoritative *Celestial Mechanics* was in the process of publication by installments), and made it known to the Irish Royal Astronomer. The consequence was that after a brilliant episode studying at Trinity College, Dublin, Hamilton himself became Irish Royal Astronomer at the age of 22. Math remained his first love, however, particularly number theory and forms of calculus.

It was in relation to what he called Icosian calculus that he began devising path-tracing problems on solid figures, to be solved mathematically. Aren't you glad I haven't asked you to do that?

Sliding coins PAGES 14–15

Shown move by move, the best answers I can achieve in each game are illustrated below.

Magic numbers 1 PAGES 16–17

The magic cross, wheel, and hexagon have many solutions, of which these are examples.

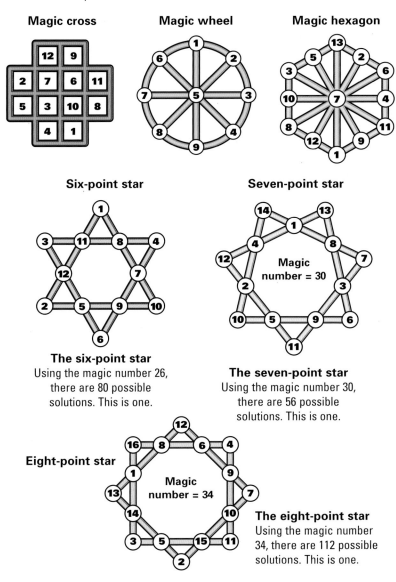

Magic cross

Magic wheel

Magic hexagon

Six-point star

The six-point star
Using the magic number 26, there are 80 possible solutions. This is one.

Seven-point star

Magic number = 30

The seven-point star
Using the magic number 30, there are 56 possible solutions. This is one.

Eight-point star

Magic number = 34

The eight-point star
Using the magic number 34, there are 112 possible solutions. This is one.

To find an optimal total for a magic star's magic number, add all the numbers to be distributed, double that, and divide by the number of points of the star.

A quicker method—which usually works—is to double the highest number and add two. (Note: It is impossible to complete a five-point star.)

About Magic numbers 1 and 2

The 3 x 3 magic square in which the numbers 1 through 9 were distributed is the earliest known of this type of problem, and has been traced back as far as 4th-century B.C. China. To the ancient Chinese, this *Lo-shu* represented either the universe or China, and its middle number therefore represented either the center of the universe or the emperor—in Chinese eyes these were effectively the same thing. Chinese mathematicians went on to construct 5 x 5 and 7 x 7 magic squares, although they found it a little more difficult with 4 x 4 and 6 x 6 squares and eventually came to regard these as ominous.

It was for its "lucky" properties that the 3 x 3 magic square became popular in the Arab world in the 10th century A.D. The associations of such squares with the universe quickly lent them religious interpretations. Sufi mystics saw the squares as representations of life in constant motion, renewed and rejuvenated by the source of power at the heart of the universal design.

The Hindus of medieval India regarded 4 x 4 and 6 x 6 magic squares as particularly potent and lucky, and went on to construct larger squares of even-numbered sides, eventually establishing a sophisticated methodology for doing so.

Magic squares finally permeated Western consciousness in the 16th century through links with Islamic countries and Hebrew interpretations in Cabalistic texts. Two centuries later, the great Swiss mathematician Leonhard Euler was fascinated by them, as was his contemporary Benjamin Franklin, who invented a type all his own.

Magic numbers 2 PAGES 18–19

Examples of answers to the magic square puzzles are shown below. There is always more than one possible answer because most puzzles remain equally valid if rows are reversed horizontally or vertically.

4 x 4 magic squares

8	-7	-6	5
-4	3	2	-1
1	-2	-3	4
-5	6	7	-8

8	-5	-6	5
-3	2	3	0
1	-2	-1	4
-4	7	6	-7

12	-1	-2	9
1	6	7	4
5	2	3	8
0	11	10	-3

1

2 Each line adds up to 2.

3 Each line totals 18.

3 x 3 magic squares

2	1	4
3	5	7
6	9	8

12	1	18
9	6	4
2	36	3

3	1	2
9	6	4
18	36	12

4 The total in each case is 5.

5 Each line totals 216.

6 Each line totals 6.

14	10	1	22	18
20	11	7	3	24
21	17	13	9	5
2	23	19	15	6
8	4	25	16	12

5 x 5 magic square

7 Each line totals 65.

Combi-cards PAGES 20–21

The sets of combi-cards should be divided and numbered as shown below.

Four cards

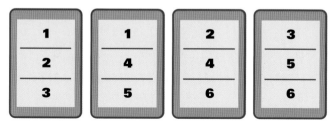

Five cards

Six cards

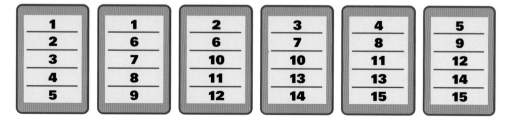

The highest numbers of these three series are 6, 10, and 15, representing a mathematical progression of:

$$\frac{4 \times 3}{2} \ (= 6) \qquad \frac{5 \times 4}{2} \ (= 10) \qquad \frac{6 \times 5}{2} \ (= 15)$$

so that the highest number on a seven-card set will be $\frac{7 \times 6}{2}$, or 21.

About Combi-cards

There is good reasoning behind the mathematical equations given as part of the answers. The highest number in each set represents:

$$\frac{\text{the number of cards x the number of numbers on each card}}{\text{the number of times each number is included (always 2)}}$$

An interestingly varied set of cards is obtained if each number on the cards is allocated a different color. For those of you who have an aversion to figures, a set of colored cards may prove a more enjoyable challenge.

Money problems PAGES 22–23

A ring of coins
Shown below is the quickest way of completing the ring.

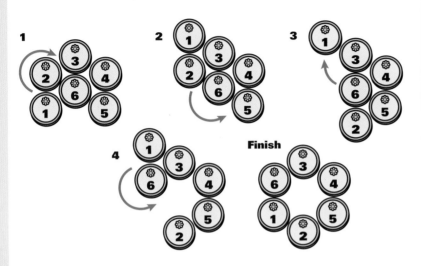

About Solitaire 1 and 2
This kind of solitaire is in essence a means of playing checkers by oneself. It is interesting to note, though, that the first recorded use of the word "solitaire" in English in reference to this game—more often called pegboard solitaire now, in order to distinguish it from the solitaire card games—occurred ten years before the publication of the first authoritative study of checkers, William Payne's *Guide to the Game of Draughts* (with a dedication written by Dr. Samuel Johnson) in 1756. It is also debatable whether, in reference to this game, it is the player who is meant to be "solitary" (the meaning of *solitaire* in French) or the single coin left at the end of a successful game.

Solitaire 1
Shown here are five moves that leave only one coin. It makes little difference which space is left free at the beginning.

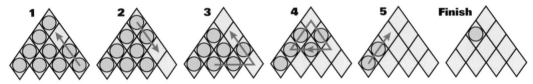

Solitaire 2
Shown here are our nine moves to complete the game.

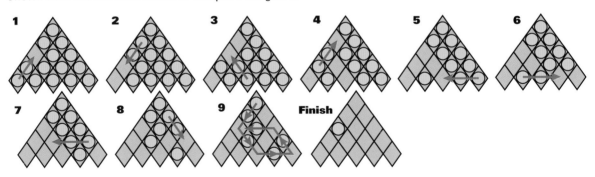

The space left free at the beginning must be the center one of any outside row of five: spaces 4, 6, or 13. These spaces are topologically equivalent, as the shape is an equilateral triangle.

The 18-point problem PAGES 24–25
Think ahead
The 11th-level problem can be solved as shown below. The 18-point problem is explained at right.

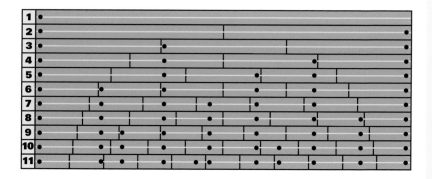

The open-ended challenge
It has been suggested, fairly authoritatively, that—even with the utmost foresight—the 17th dot is the farthest that anyone can ordinarily get. Well, I gave you a chance to get to the 18th, anyway. Maybe it takes a microscope to be able to go farther still.

The real reason is, however, by that stage the vertical lines are clustering so thickly, each space between them "moving" either toward the center or toward the edges, that any specific space has in fact traveled right across previous borders and *into the next*.

Jumping coins PAGES 26–27
Game 1
With six counters, the solution can be reached in 15 moves. See below.

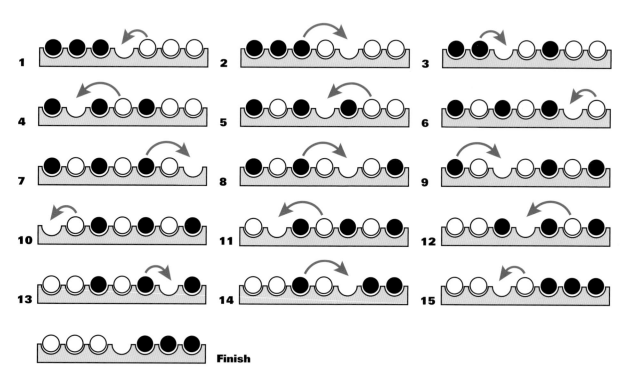

Finish

Game 2 PAGES 26–27

With eight counters, the solution can be reached in 24 moves. See below.

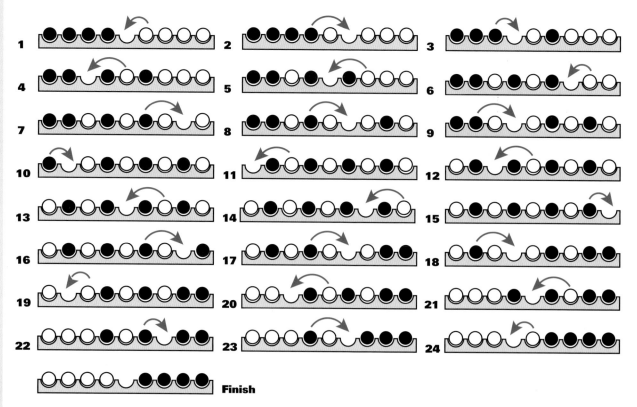

Finish

Game 3

With ten counters, the solution can be reached in 35 moves. The pattern for solving this game is illustrated move by move for Games 1 and 2. These moves can be summarized by a formula as shown here. In Game 1, using six counters, the sequence starts with one move by either of the center counters into the middle space. It is then followed by two moves by counters of the other type, then three moves from the first type, three moves again from the second type, and then back again with three moves, then two moves, then one move. The total number of moves for each game can be calculated by adding the sequence shown. Mathematically, the minimum number of moves can be seen as: y (half the number of counters) x (y + 2). Thus Game 1: 3 x 5 = 15; Game 2: 4 x 6 = 24; Game 3: 5 x 7 = 35.

Game 1

$1 + 2 + 3 + 3 + 3 + 2 + 1$ = 15

Game 2

$1 + 2 + 3 + 4 + 4 + 4 + 3 + 2 + 1$ = 24

Game 3

$1 + 2 + 3 + 4 + 5 + 5 + 5 + 4 + 3 + 2 + 1$ = 35

Life or death PAGES 28–29

Outer ring

Congratulations on becoming emperor of Rome! It was brilliant of you and your proposed co-candidate to take up positions 13 and 28 in the circle of 40.

Inner ring

If you have arranged things correctly, the lion's lunch should have been numbers 4, 10, 15, 20, 26, and 30 in the original circle of 36.

The mathematical formula for solving such problems has eluded mathematicians for centuries. Practical solutions are best achieved by trial and error.

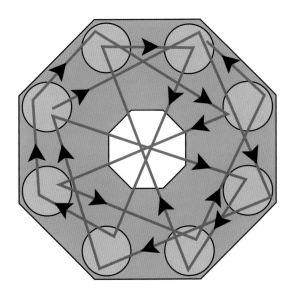

From pillar to post PAGES 30–31

Courtyard challenge

The theoretical maximum number of lines I could have run along is 20. No matter how many different ways I tried to run, I could never get beyond 17. If the courtyard had had seven or even nine pillars, however, the full complement would have been easier to achieve. I realized that for reasons of topology the full complement of 20 continuous tracks is impossible. The general rule is that if there are more than two nodes from which an odd number of lines emerge, the network cannot be completed with a continuous line ... and each of the eight nodes of the courtyard has a possible five lines emerging from it.

Posting the mail

The strategy by which the right hand can always win is simple to follow. If the left hand starts with one newspaper in one mailbox, the right hand puts two in the two mailboxes opposite. If the left hand starts with two papers in two boxes, the right then puts just one in the opposite box. (Because there are 13 boxes, one box can be opposite two, and vice versa.) Either way, after this opening response, the right hand merely repeats whatever the left hand does, and always gets the last move.

Gridlock PAGE 32

You can cross town like this (among other possible routes). What a complicated journey!

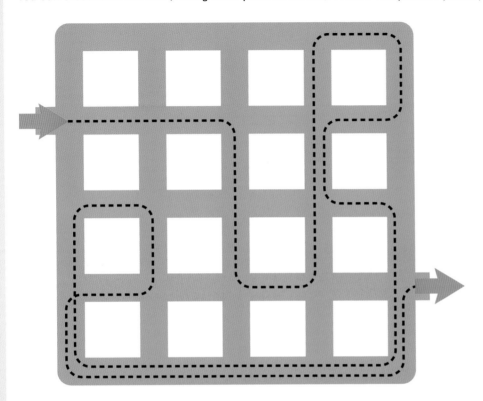

Crossroads PAGE 33

Here, cream indicates a coin's starting point, and red indicates its finishing point. The trick is to remember that each time you place a coin on a circle to move to a successive one, that circle is to be the final destination of the next coin. There will always be one pathway free using this strategy.

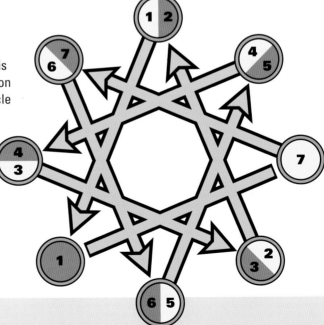

Separate and connect PAGES 34–35

Cutting the necklace

Make your cuts on each side of the fourth pearl and on each side of the eleventh pearl; then you have the sequence: 1 to 3, 4, 5 to 10, 11, 12 to 23. This represents lengths of: 3 pearls, 1 pearl, 6 pearls, 1 pearl, 12 pearls; from which it is possible to make up any number between 1 and 23.

Factorial forty

The numbers are 1, 3, 9, and 27.

1	= 1		9 + 3 − 1	= 11	
3 − 1	= 2		9 + 3	= 12	
3	= 3		9 + 3 + 1	= 13	
3 + 1	= 4		27 − 9 − 3 − 1	= 14	
9 − 3 − 1	= 5		27 − 9 − 3	= 15	
9 − 3	= 6		27 − 9 − 3 + 1	= 16	
9 − 3 + 1	= 7		27 − 9 − 1	= 17	
9 − 1	= 8		27 − 9	= 18	
9	= 9		27 − 9 + 1	= 19	
9 + 1	= 10		27 − 9 + 3 − 1	= 20	

27 − 9 + 3	= 21		27 + 3 + 1	= 31	
27 − 9 + 3 + 1	= 22		27 + 9 − 3 − 1	= 32	
27 − 3 − 1	= 23		27 + 9 − 3	= 33	
27 − 3	= 24		27 + 9 − 3 + 1	= 34	
27 − 3 + 1	= 25		27 + 9 − 1	= 35	
27 − 1	= 26		27 + 9	= 36	
27	= 27		27 + 9 + 1	= 37	
27 + 1	= 28		27 + 9 + 3 − 1	= 38	
27 + 3 − 1	= 29		27 + 9 + 3	= 39	
27 + 3	= 30		27 + 9 + 3 + 1	= 40	

Missing links

$1 + 2 + 3 − 4 + 5 + 6 + 78 + 9 = 100$

About Missing links

A line of figures 1 through 9 followed by another figure that ends in a zero reminds us immediately of how securely our numeric system is based on the number ten. Although the decimal system now seems entirely familiar to us, other systems in other times have been based on other numbers. Historical evidence that the decimal system once meant far less than it does today may be observed in the way we measure time (in 60s or 12s), define angles (in 60s, basically), or even sell eggs (in 12s); even one's life span is said to be measured as though carving notches on a tally-stick— "three *score* years and ten," following the practice of notching up a score for every 20.

By the way, if in my introduction to this puzzle I had said it was possible that *three* of the numbers in the equation should have been printed as a single number, your answer could have been:

$123 − 4 − 5 − 6 − 7 + 8 − 9 = 100$

If I had not limited the symbols to be inserted to plus or minus signs, another solution could have been:

$12 + 34 + (5 \times 6) + 7 + 8 + 9 = 100.$

The Tower of Brahma PAGES 36–37

Shifting positions

With four counters it takes 15 moves, as shown below.

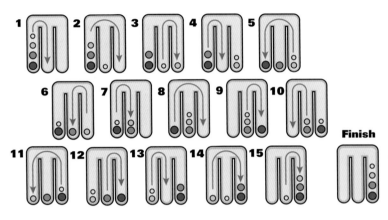

With three counters it takes seven moves. With five counters it would take 31 moves. With 64 counters it would take more or less forever.

The legend

Let's be more precise. With 64 disks the number of moves necessary to move the tower is 18,446,744,073,709,551,615. And at one per second, that would take around 585 billion years—not actually forever, perhaps, but more than a hundred times the duration of the universe as presently calculated.

The formula for calculating the number of moves required is $2^n - 1$, where n = the number of disks. For 3 disks, this gives $2^3 - 1 = 7$; for 4 disks, $2^4 - 1 = 15$; for 5 disks, $2^5 - 1 = 31$; and for 64 disks, $2^{64} - 1$, which is the very large number given above.

Interplanetary courier PAGES 38–39

This is how my trips can be organized. It takes only seven trips.
All four of us begin at the spaceport:

Spaceport	Space Liner
Rigellian	
Denebian	
Terrestrial	
Courier (Me)	

1 I take the Denebian up to the liner:

Rigellian	Denebian
Terrestrial ⟶	Courier

2 I return alone:

Rigellian	Denebian
Terrestrial ⟵	
Courier	

3 I take the Rigellian up to the liner:

Terrestrial	Rigellian
⟶	Denebian
	Courier

4 I return with the Denebian:

Denebian	
Terrestrial ⟵	Rigellian
Courier	

5 I take the Terrestrial up to the liner:

Denebian	Rigellian
⟶	Terrestrial
	Courier

6 I return alone:

Denebian ⟵	Rigellian
Courier	Terrestrial

7 I take the Denebian up to the liner:

	Rigellian
	Denebian
⟶	Terrestrial
	Courier

And we all go through the airlock, into the tender care of the hostesses.

Husbands and wives PAGES 40–41

Island	Crossings	Mainland
	Initial situation	
Mr. A, Mrs. A		
Mr. B, Mrs. B		
Mr. C, Mrs. C		
	First crossing to mainland Mr. A, Mrs. A	
Mr. B, Mrs. B		
Mr. C, Mrs. C	⟶	
	Second crossing to island Mrs. A	Mr. A
Mr. B, Mrs. B		
Mr. C, Mrs. C	⟵	
	Third crossing to mainland Mrs. A, Mrs. B	Mr. A
Mr. B		
Mr. C, Mrs. C	⟶	
	Fourth crossing to island Mrs. B	Mr. A, Mrs. A
Mr. B		
Mr. C, Mrs. C	⟵	
	Fifth crossing to mainland Mr. B, Mrs. B	Mr. A, Mrs. A
Mr. C, Mrs. C	⟶	
	Sixth crossing to island Mrs. B	Mr. A, Mrs. A Mr. B
Mr. C, Mrs. C	⟵	
	Seventh crossing to mainland Mrs. B, Mrs. C	Mr. A, Mrs. A Mr. B
Mr. C	⟶	
	Eighth crossing to island Mrs. C	Mr. A, Mrs. A Mr. B, Mrs. B
Mr. C	⟵	
	Ninth crossing to mainland Mr. C, Mrs. C	Mr. A, Mrs. A Mr. B, Mrs. B
	⟶	

About Husbands and wives

This is just one of many such problems relating to couples who are presented as inseparable in some way. Similar puzzles involving more than three couples require a boat that will hold more than two people at a time, however. For four or five couples, a boat that will take three people at a time is a necessity; and for six or more couples, a four-seater boat is essential if the rules of inseparability as laid down here are to be followed.

The octopus handshake PAGES 42–43

The disks meet at even numbers, then odd numbers, as shown below in Game 1. In Game 2 they will meet at identical numbers when rotated as shown.

Game 1

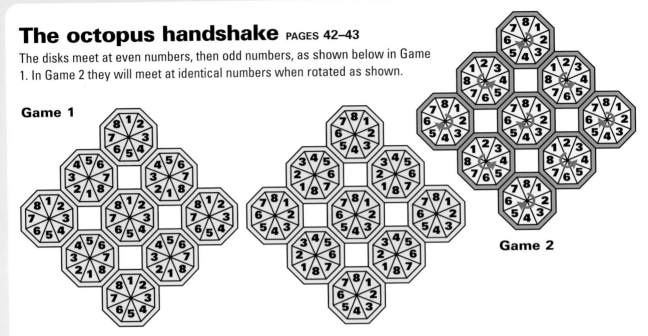

Game 2

Game 3

Our octopuses have experimented many times to find the most convenient way to work through all the possible combinations of eight-tentacle contact. They finally struck on what is probably the easiest method: One of them stays still, tentacles outstretched and unmoving; the other then methodically works through every combination possible. This can be calculated by the following multiplication, known

as factorial 8: 1 x 2 x 3 x 4 x 5 x 6 x 7 x 8, which comes to 40,320 alltogether. At 12 moves a minute it comes to 56 hours nonstop! There is no need for the static octopus to go through the whole routine as well—all the possible combinations have been done.

On the other tentacle, if no tentacle is to touch another more than once, the number of total possible combinations is reduced to 8 x 8, which is 64.

Calculating the odds

PAGES **44–45**

Pascal's Triangle

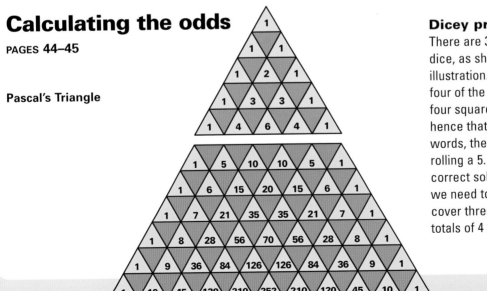

Dicey problems

There are 36 possibilities for two dice, as shown in the question illustration. A 1:9 chance equates to four of the 36 squares. We note that four squares have the number 5, hence that is one solution. In other words, there is a 1:9 chance of rolling a 5. Similarly 9 is also a correct solution. For a 1:12 chance we need to find the totals that cover three squares. These are the totals of 4 and 10.

Up in the air PAGES 46–47

There are 52 possible outcomes, so the odds that all five will drop either into separate tubs or together all into one tub are both 1:52. If you carried the process out in practice once a week, this outcome would result on average once a year.

The odds on the five balls falling into three tubs are 25:52, or almost 1:2. This is due to the fact that there are ten possible outcomes of balls in a 1 + 1 + 3 formation, and 15 of balls in a 2 + 2 + 1 formation—a total of 25 landing in three tubs.

In a 4 + 1 formation there are only five possibilities (shown mathematically as: 1 + 2345, 2 + 1345, 3 + 1245, 4 + 1235, 5 +1234) so the odds are 5:52, or between 1:10 and 1:11.

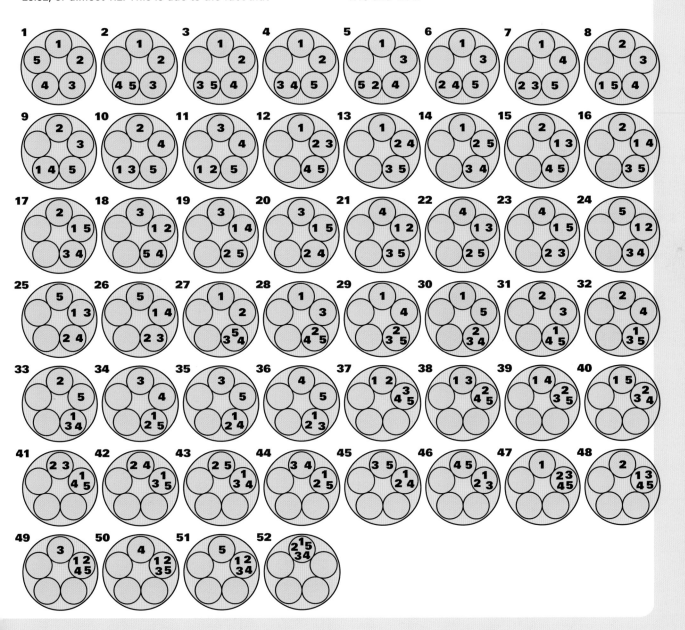

Lucky spinner, lucky dice PAGES 48–49

Game 1

In a series of spins, with each spinner matched against one other, spinner A is the most successful.

Out of 100 spins between A and B, spinner A beats spinner B 56 times. This is because value 2 occupies 56% of the area of spinner B and so whenever the pointer of spinner B registers 2, spinner A, with value 3, wins. In terms of probability this is referred to as 0.56 probability. (Probability of 1 is certainty; of 0 is the opposite.)

Similarly, spinner A also beats spinner C, but only 51 times out of 100, as 51% of spinner C has a value less than spinner A. The probability in this case is 0.51.

If all spinners compete simultaneously, however, the chances of spinner A winning are dramatically reduced; in fact it is the worst choice. This is because the separate probabilities of spinner A beating the others must be combined, and 0.56 x 0.51 = 0.28, which means that out of 100 spins, spinner A would win only 28 times.

Game 2

When two six-sided dice are thrown at the same time, there are 36 possible outcomes, as we saw on page 45 (**Dicey problems**). Taking dice A and B, therefore, we can see that 24 times out of 36, A will show value 4, therefore beating the value 3 of B (which appears 36 times). With B and C, value 2 of C appears 24 times, allowing B to win. With C and D, the answer is also 24. The fact that C beats D is shown in diagrammatic form below. A similar table can be completed to show that D beats A 24 out of 36 times too.

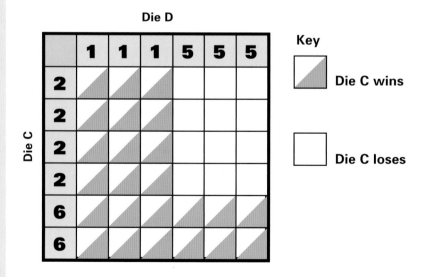

110

Hidden shapes PAGES 50–51

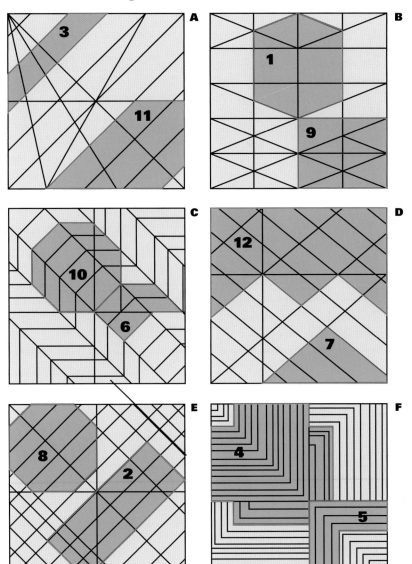

About Hidden shapes

One form of camouflage—and one that is observable in nature generally—is that which allows a gentle blurring of outlines, a simple fading into the background. Another, featured in these puzzles, is the deliberate creation of dominant patterns that distract the eye in a number of ways so that shapes within the patterns are rendered less obvious. Here we are confronted by a multitude of redundant lines that attract the attention by their geometrical regularity or angularity; by areas of color and shading that create their own forms; and finally by a number of shapes within the patterns that are misleadingly close—but not identical—to those being sought.

Match the lines PAGE 52

The deliberate errors are: A6, B4, C2, D2, D3, D6, E3, E4, F3, G1, G3.

Square the match PAGE 53

	Change 2 matches	Change 3 matches	Change 4 matches
Create 2 squares			
Create 3 squares			
Create 4 squares			
Create 5 squares			

About Square the match

As with many match problems, the trick is to visualize the correct final form before moving any matches at all. Some, for example, end up in squares of different sizes, some overlap, and many have common sides. But this is not to say that the trial-and-error approach cannot succeed: For most people it is the only way to reach the solutions you need. Moreover, by actually moving the matches—or drawing the moves on paper—it is possible to work toward the solutions to these puzzles, to progress toward an understanding of what size of squares you are looking for, and to see if any should overlap. With this experience it is entirely possible for most people to go on to devise their own more complex puzzles to test their friends.

Tracks and traces PAGES 54–55

Only shapes 2, 3, 5, 6, 8, 9, 10, and 11 can be traced around without taking pencil from paper, as shown below. Of those, only 3, 6, 8, 9, and 11 end at the starting point.

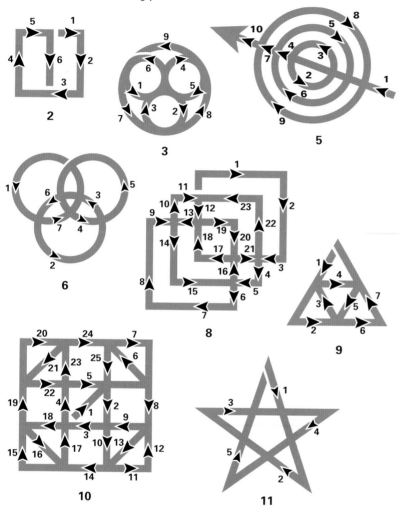

About Tracks and traces

A famous problem also based on the possibility or impossibility of a single continuous line connecting a complex circuit concerns the seven bridges in and around the town of Königsberg.

The townspeople were said for centuries never to have been able to solve the question: Could they go for a stroll, crossing each bridge only once, and end up where they began?

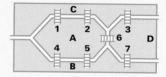

Königsberg bridges

The eminent 18th-century Swiss mathematician Leonhard Euler eventually proved that it could not be done. To do so, he constructed thematic drawings posing the same problem geometrically.

Drawn below in this way are two modern versions of the same problem that are thus said to have "topological equivalence" to the original. In all of them, from the original physical problem onward, if you were allowed just one break in the sequence—if having crossed the third bridge you could start from somewhere else toward the fourth—you would be able to cross all seven points and find yourself where you started.

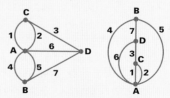

Topological equivalents

Impossible traces

Shapes 4 and 7 cannot be successfully traced. They are both versions of the "impossible" shape shown on page 55.

The general rule is that if there are more than two junctions with an odd number of tracks, the route cannot be traced. If there are two odd-number junctions, the design can be regarded as borderline: If it can be traced, the line will not end at the starting point. Choosing the right starting point is an important key to discovering the trace.

Count the cubes PAGES 56–57

Game 1

1 – 40 cubes
2 – 30 cubes
3 – 38 cubes
4 – 58 cubes
5 – 18 cubes
6 – 20 cubes
7 – 18 cubes
8 – 56 cubes

Game 2

Your score box should look like the chart below. The visual clue suggested on page 57 is to turn the page upside down, which makes the missing cubes appear solid.

S C O R E B O X	1	2	3	4	5
MISSING CUBES	26	19	20	7	36
CUBES COLORED ON THREE SIDES	1	1	1	1	1
CUBES COLORED ON TWO SIDES	6	6	6	3	10
CUBES COLORED ON ONE SIDE	12	12	12	3	19
NOT COLORED	7	0	1	0	6

About Count the cubes

These problems depend on our perception of depth, the three-dimensional effect afforded by perspective, in two dimensions. So well is this effect now understood—although it was either unknown or ignored for millennia before medieval times—that computers can be programmed to recognize three-dimensional objects (such as a particular programmer's facial features in any expression) at any angle. Equally, holograms are not merely works of art to marvel at, but are used for commercial and security purposes. Yet it is also well known that perspective can be misleading. Most of us at one time or another have seen the carefully constructed room scenario in which a person who crosses the floor from left to right appears to shrink. In such an instance the room is not, in fact, square at all, and by walking from left to right the person is really walking steadily away from the viewpoint.

No such tricks are included in these puzzles. All the same, as I implied in my second question, there is a visual shortcut to the answer that is a direct result of the vagaries of perspective. Hold the book upside down: Most people will now see the missing cubes as the only solid cubes—which are naturally much easier to count. The painted cubes now appear as a sort of tiled surround.

Dividing the square PAGES 58–59

If you shaded in the halves and quarters, there is always the danger that you would count one variant and its opposite as separate ways of dividing the square.

The six ways of dividing a 4 x 4 grid square in half are:

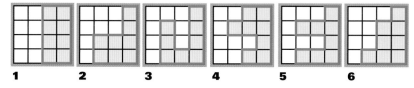

1   **2**   **3**   **4**   **5**   **6**

The five ways of dividing a 4 x 4 grid square in quarters are:

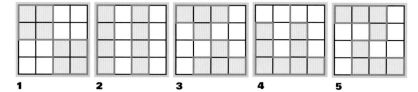

1   **2**   **3**   **4**   **5**

About Dividing the square

The final game shows only 36 ways of dividing a 6 x 6 square into four congruent parts. However, more than 96 possibilities exist, all in four variants of each theme (in rotations and mirror images); there is also inevitably one final method of division, the simplest possible, into four squares of 3 x 3 each. This has to remain an individual variant, because it looks the same whether rotated or as a mirror image.

You may like to continue, by careful analysis and progression, to work out all the other variants.

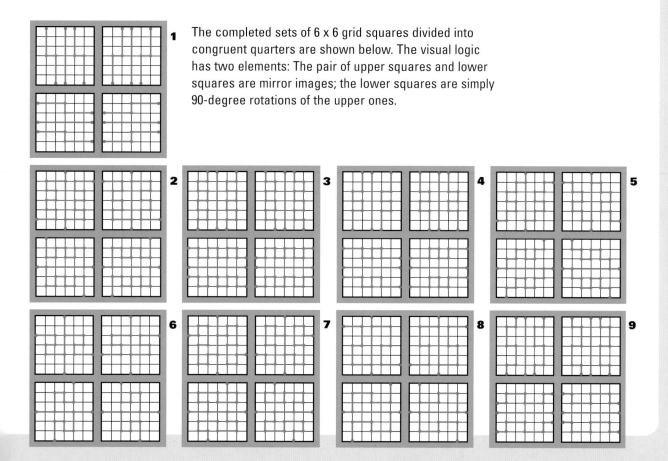

1 The completed sets of 6 x 6 grid squares divided into congruent quarters are shown below. The visual logic has two elements: The pair of upper squares and lower squares are mirror images; the lower squares are simply 90-degree rotations of the upper ones.

Cube problems PAGES 60–61

Game 1

Keeping one cube still, while the other turns, allows 24 variations. Rotating both cubes, the variations possible total 24 x 24 = 576.

Game 2

Similarly—and as long as the cubes remain in the same order—the variations possible with three cubes therefore total 24 x 24 x 24 = 13,824.

Game 3

As long as the cubes within the formation of eight keep to the same positional arrangement—and counting a single turn of one face of one cube as a variation of the whole pattern—then the number of ways the whole pattern can be changed is 24 times itself eight times or 110,075,314,176.

Game 4

This is what the die should have looked like with the missing symbols filled in:

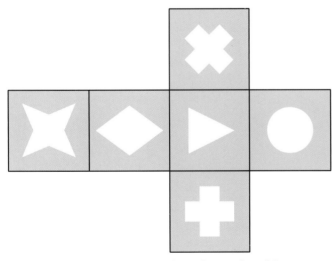

The different die, sneakily, was the only one that did not feature a blank space. But its symbols as shown simply will not fit with the other views of the "true" die.

About Cube problems Games 1, 2, and 3

Changing the order of the three cubes and the eight cubes multiplies the factorial figure by the number of variations then possible in each case.

For example, with three cubes there are three possible different arrangements of the cubes (ABC, BAC, and ACB—the other three possibilities merely reverse each of these and are not therefore statistically important). And for each of these orders there are 13,824 variations. So the actual total possible in these circumstances is 3 x 13,824 = 41,472.

You may like to go on to work out in exactly the same fashion the total number of variations possible with the eight cubes, given that there are 20,160 different positional arrangements of eight cubes in this formation. The answer is something greater than 2.219×10^{15}.

Game 4

This puzzle is made particularly difficult because the "normal" situation, in which three sides of each cube would allow the others to be deduced straightforwardly, is confused by the faces deliberately left blank. The false trail of the extraneous dice adds to the confusion. The problem can only be solved by forming known pairs of sides and building up the complete picture from these.

Pegboards PAGE 61

Game 1
There are 20 squares made up of five different sizes, as shown.

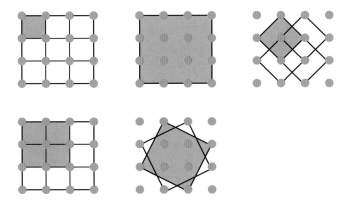

About Pegboards
For many people the most difficult part of these problems is keeping count. The first game in particular requires the ability to categorize sufficiently to be able to separate all the forms in each pattern that are of a certain size, before proceeding to count all those in the same pattern of the next size. Some people are considerably better at this than others—possibly through experience.

Variations in scale are also problematical in the second and third games, particularly in relation to squares that do not have a horizontal base.

Game 2
You can create 21 squares as shown.

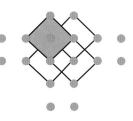

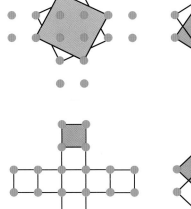

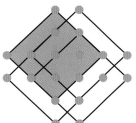

Game 3
The six pegs to remove are:

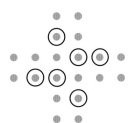

Inside-outside PAGES 62–63

The answers for the total area of the figures can be checked by simple mathematics. The formula for the area of a square, rectangle, or rhombus is length of base x vertical height, and for a circle it is pi (π = 3.142) x radius squared. For a triangle it is base x height divided by 2. The pentagon and octagon can be divided into triangles, of which the areas can be calculated, then multiplied by 5 or 6 respectively.

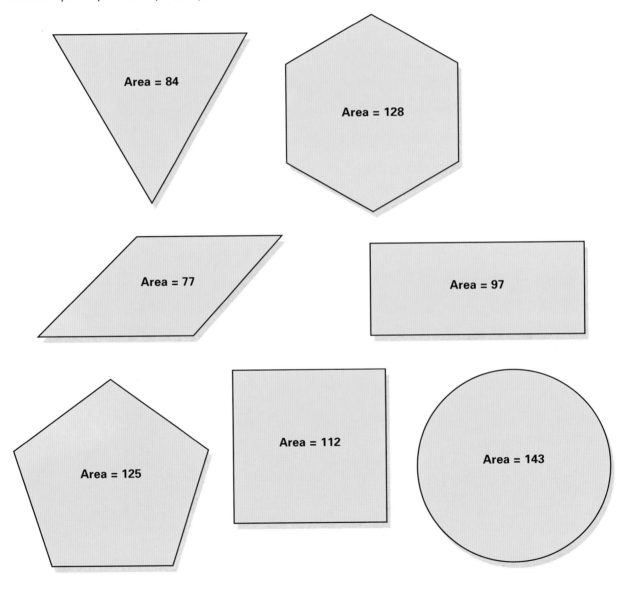

Area = 84

Area = 128

Area = 77

Area = 97

Area = 125

Area = 112

Area = 143

Repli-tiles 1 PAGES 64–65

The T-polygon contains 16 miniatures, and the stepped polygon contains 36.

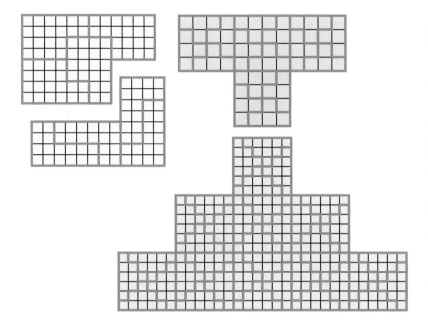

About Repli-tiles 1 and 2

Most of us have seen a kitchen floor covered in tiles in a checkerboard pattern, alternating black and white squares in a geometrical pattern. Many of us, I imagine, have also seen similarly regular pieces of mosaic or parquet work. The design is not always formed from squares, of course. Diamonds, triangles, rhombuses, and hexagons are also suitable for covering an area decoratively. And the art of doing so is called tessellation.

Except for four-sided patterns, however, it is rare for such tessellations to cover a regular area exactly; usually there are some half- or quarter-patterns left over around the edges. It is rarer still for tesseral patterns to combine to make larger versions of themselves, as the ones shown in these puzzles do.

Tessellation tends to be rare in nature, too. Probably the only field in which it occurs relatively often is in the structure of crystals.

Repli-tiles 2 PAGES 66–67

Game 1

There are eight crabs caught up in the net. See the two different patterns, right:

Game 2

Eighteen fish have been caught in the net.

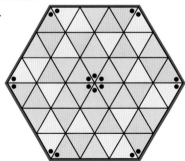

Game 3

Nine fish of the smaller variety fit exactly into the larger fish. This is also a self-replicating shape.

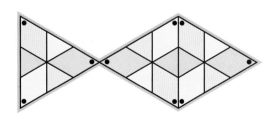

On the rebound PAGES 68–69

The paths of the rebounding balls are shown below. The impossible shot is on table B of Game 3.

Game 1

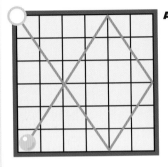 A

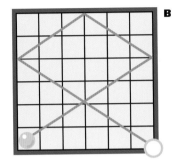 B

Game 2

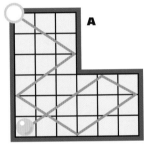 A

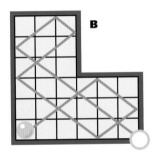 B

Game 3

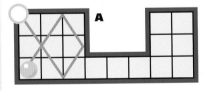 A

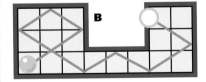 B

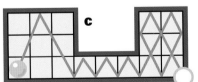 C

Impossible shot

About On the rebound

The impossible shot is Grid B of Game 3. After seven bounces the ball nearly reaches the pocket—but not quite. Accurate calculation proves this, but if you drew the line freehand the temptation to make the ball reach the pocket would almost certainly have been too great and you would have persuaded yourself that it was possible after all.

For these games I have carefully stated that the ball may travel for as long as is necessary to reach the pocket. But in a real pool game, of course, other factors intrude and have to be considered as additional hazards by each player. Having been set in motion, a ball decelerates and eventually comes to a standstill (unless it drops into a pocket first) through the effects of friction against the cloth surface and of the loss of momentum caused by rebounding off a cushion.

It is possible to introduce the idea of such an "entropy" factor into these games by speculating how many of the puzzles can still be solved if, for instance, the initial speed of the ball is reduced by a proportion (say 2%) for every grid square wholly or partly crossed (giving, therefore, a maximum total of 50 squares crossed), and by a greater proportion (say 10%) for every bounce. (You may choose whatever percentage proportions you think suitable, naturally.)

Further mathematical considerations may also be introduced at your discretion to represent such effects as putting spin on the ball.

A piece of cake PAGES 70–71

Because many rings of the segments in a three-segment cake interconnect with several others, at least six numbers or colors are required. The design of the coloration of the four-segment cake is inevitable, following the rules. The other cakes are drawn and numbered for you as shown here.

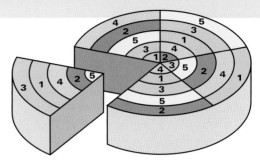

Five-segment, five-ring cake

Cake 1

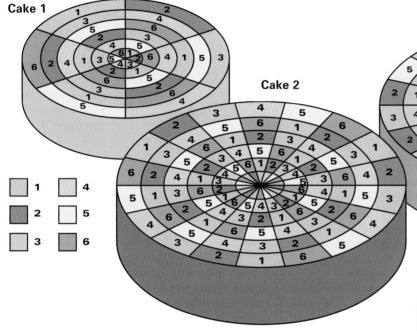

Cake 2

Cake 3

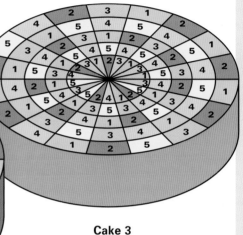

- 1
- 2
- 3
- 4
- 5
- 6

The hollow cube PAGES 72–73

The correct patterns are revealed below. Did you manage to deduce the 8 x 8 stylized capital M in Game 2? The views do not give any information for the top six squares of the grid, which apart from the stylized capital M provide a further seven possible solutions.

Game 1

Game 2

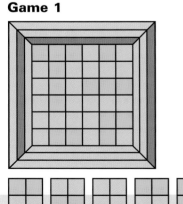
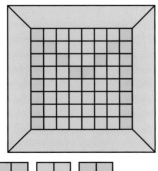

About The hollow cube

These puzzles depend just as much on logic as they do on observation. Logic is required to sort out the evidence and to make enough sense of it to be able to fill in as much of the answer panel as there is information. But in the second puzzle the information is not all there, making logic essential in order to deduce a symmetrical solution. I am emphasizing the need for logic here because it is often the case that particularly observant or particularly logical people are perplexed (or at least inhibited) if there is an element of the puzzle that is unknown and therefore requires deduction (or intuitive guessing) to be used at the same time as more "mechanical" logic.

How many? PAGES 74–75
The answer to each puzzle is shown in the boxes.

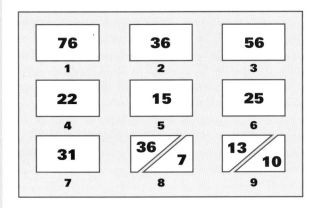

See **Pegboards** answer on page 117 for further explanation.

Cubes and routes PAGES 76–77
The solutions to the three-dimensional cubes are listed below.

Game 1

ANSWERS			
THREE PAIRS	1,6	4,9	7,8
GROUP OF THREE		2,5,10	
ODD ONE OUT		3	

Game 2

DISTANCES	
HAND NO. 1	26
HAND NO. 2	30
FOOT NO. 1	37
FOOT NO. 2	38

About Cubes and routes

The very fact that the same thing can look totally different from a different viewpoint—so that our perception of it is altered although our awareness that it remains the same is constant—is often exploited by realist painters, particularly painters of outdoor and natural scenes. Many, before declaring a painting finished, survey the subject again through a mirror or by turning their back on the subject and bending over, even looking through their own legs, thus obtaining a different view of the subject they have just painted. By doing so, they get a new idea of salient features of the subject that they may then wish to add to the work.

Such aspects of perception prove that the conscious mind works in three-dimensional images, stored and related for use in categorizing and memorizing everything we see, and generally available to recall in such a way as to make comparison and recognition possible, even from unfamiliar angles. In fact, we make use of this faculty every moment of our waking experience—and, if someone loses it (as occasionally happens following accident or disease), everyday life becomes devastatingly complicated.

Game 2
The robot can also be treated as a game for two players: One races from Hand 1 to Foot 1, the other from Hand 2 to Foot 2—but no cube can be occupied by more than one player, and a cube once used is out of bounds to both players until the end of the game. Some fairly vicious tactics of blocking and evasion are possible…

Find the polygons PAGES 78–79

As you can see below, the number of possible shapes that can be found within this simply constructed pattern is almost limitless.

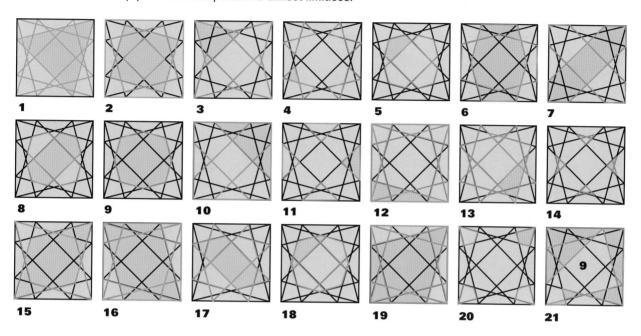

Multi-views PAGES 80–81

The 16 views are combined correctly in the table below.

A	E	I	M
2	**7**	**3**	**4**
B	**F**	**J**	**N**
6	**5**	**10**	**16**
C	**G**	**K**	**O**
9	**1**	**8**	**14**
D	**H**	**L**	**P**
12	**13**	**15**	**11**

About Multi-views

These problems combine spatial awareness with logic—the ability to visualize in three dimensions from two-dimensional views.

In fact, the overhead views and front views given correspond fairly well to what architects call a plan and a front elevation. The plan represents the shape as laid out horizontally on the ground—the elevation is a front view that is derived exactly and immediately from the dimensions of the plan. Other elevations derived by architects in the same way are those of the remaining sides of the building, each seen as a direct face-on view, with no perspective.

Distortrix 1 PAGES 82–83

The distorted image is reproduced
for all the shapes, below.

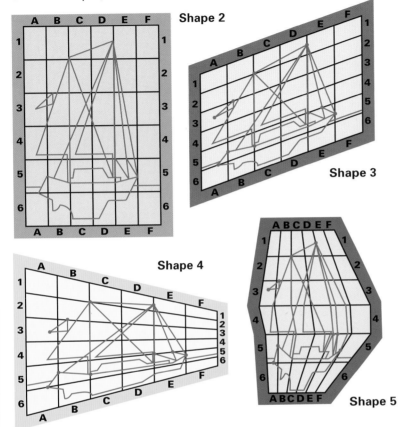

Shape 2

Shape 3

Shape 4

Shape 5

About Distortrix 1 and 2

Toward the end of the 19th century there was considerable debate, in the light of the revelations made by Charles Darwin, over whether evolution in fact also worked on the principles of distortion from one original "plan" of a creature to its next evolved stage. Much of the discussion was spurious, but the fact remains that evolution has in many cases progressed in a way that does indeed correspond closely to a distorted framework. (On the other hand, there are even more cases in nature where two creatures that bear some resemblance in form—different sizes, perhaps, or one a longer, thinner version of the other—are not in reality closely related by evolution.)

It may interest you to create further distortions that can be resolved by using a cylindrical mirror (which it is not too difficult to make from a length of shiny foil wrapped around a household cardboard tube). The curved shape required is the one seen on page 85, which can of course itself be utilized for this purpose in conjunction with a reflecting cylinder of the same diameter as the central near-circle.

Distortrix 2

PAGES 84–85

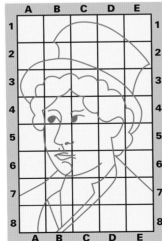

Shape 1

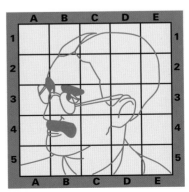

Shape 2

Space filler PAGES 86–87

Game 1

The smallest number of equilateral triangles into which the large triangle can be divided using the triangles of the grid is 11.

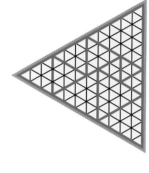
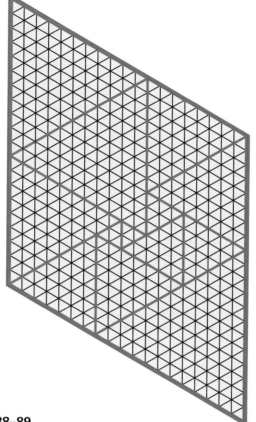

About Space filler

These puzzles again reflect the principles of tessellation (see **Replitiles**, pages 64–67)—covering a regular area with a regular pattern that may or may not be related in shape. But here it is not the tessellation that is important so much as the concept of filling the area using the lines of that tessellation (which may be helpful or unhelpful) as a guide.

Game 2

The smallest number of equilateral triangles into which the 19 x 20 grid parallelogram can be divided is 13.

Subways PAGES 88–89

Line diagrams of the subways show the shortest routes for each problem.

Game 1

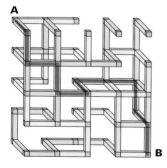

A to B = 13

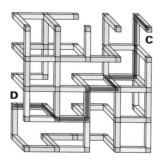

C to D = 13

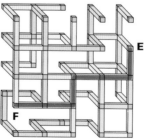

E to F = 8

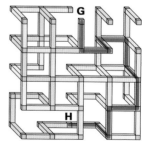

G to H = 15

Game 2

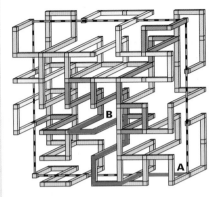

A to B = 13

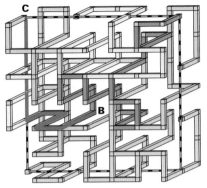

B to C = 10

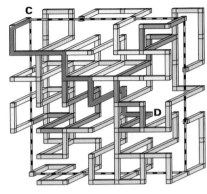

C to D = 13

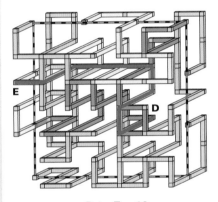

D to E = 12

About Subways

More complex versions of both these games can be played by imagining that one or another line is out of service. Both can also be played competitively by two or more players, who start at points apparently equidistant from an agreed destination. The race begins, taking alternate moves, station by station and where appropriate remaining for two or three turns (when changing lines). No station can be occupied by more than one player; when blocked in this way a player must nevertheless make a move, even if it has to be backward.

You may devise your own subway line systems following similar principles.

Computer patterns PAGES 90–91

The growing screen pattern is revealed opposite. If the rules are not followed strictly, however, different patterns result.

The patterns explained

It's very easy, when working out these patterns, to reinterpret the rules slightly to reach what you think the next stage *ought* to be. If the patterns you have created differ from the ones shown here, this could be the reason, so read the rules again carefully.

The pattern is generated and transformed as cells change color and as new cells are added. Bear in mind that:

A New cells *cannot* grow if the blank they would grow in is touched by existing cells on more than one side, even if the existing touching cells are pale green and so will disappear at the instant of the new cell's birth.

B A game starts with an initial configuration. In the illustrated game, this is the single, central dark green cell. It could be any number of cells, however, in any pattern in any part of the screen.

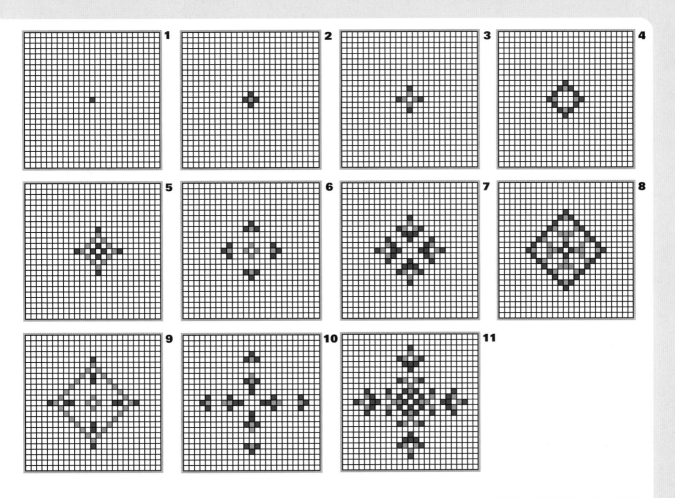

About Computer patterns

Once you know the rules by heart, such growth patterns can become almost addictive in their fascination: It becomes difficult not to want to see what the next pattern looks like. Every sheet of squared paper in the house quickly becomes occupied by crystallate designs, and enthusiasts have been known to stay up late at night cursing as pens gradually run dry. The simplicity of a single set of rules applied strictly and logically over and over is almost hypnotic—and some of the results are beautiful, especially as the designs get bigger and more complex. (I can personally recommend stages 12, 13 [shown below], 17, 21, 24, 25, and every stage thereafter to anyone who has the patience.)

Alternatively, if the rules are changed slightly—for instance, if growth occurs only from second generation (pale green) squares—different growth patterns immediately emerge. In every case, for success the rules must be precisely defined (and understood) and rigidly adhered to. Another interesting variation is to start from a different, more complex, initial configuration (such as a bilaterally symmetrical pattern or even an asymmetrical one) or configurations— two at different corners, for example.

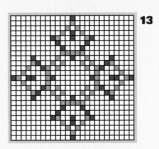